Momentous Decisions in Missions Today

DONALD A. McGAVRAN

BAKER BOOK HOUSE
Grand Rapids, Michigan 49506

Copyright 1984 by
Baker Book House Company

ISBN: 0-8010-6176-8

Library of Congress Catalog Card Number: 84-72121

Printed in the United States of America

The author wishes to express his appreciation for permission to
reprint "Is the Great Commission God's Command?" by Everett F.
Harrison, from *Christianity Today* (November 23, 1973), copyright 1973
by *Christianity Today*.

Chapter 15, "Unchain Missionary Societies," appeared in abbreviated form
under the title "Have We Shackled Missions to the National Church?" in
Eternity (December 1982). Chapter 21, "New Faces of the Urban Church,"
is taken primarily from an article by the same title in *Urban Mission*
(September 1983) and is used by kind permission.

Unless otherwise noted, Scripture quotations are from the New American
Standard Bible, © The Lockman Foundation 1960, 1962, 1963, 1968, 1971,
1972, 1973, 1975, and are used by permission. Other versions
cited are the Revised Standard Version (RSV), the King
James Version (KJV), the Good News Bible (GNB), and The Bible: A
New Translation (*Moffatt*).

Contents

Introduction

In the rapidly changing world of the closing years of the twentieth century, missions ought to make numerous momentous decisions. How missions ought to carry out their basic purpose is defined differently by the missions and denominations concerned in every piece of the vast mosaic of mankind. The whole field, therefore, bristles with momentous questions.

Three groups of Christians must answer these questions: ministers and practicing Christians of the sending and receiving Churches;[1] executives of the hundreds of missionary societies; and missionaries who go overseas as special messengers of God's grace. World evangelism presents different tasks to each group; yet all three ought to think through three questions:

1. In the world of today and tomorrow what does God command concerning world evangelization?
2. How effectively is this command being carried out in each piece of the mosaic for which we are responsible?
3. How can it be carried out more effectively?

1. The word *Churches* (with a capital *C*) refers to denominations, as the Church Universal. Written with a small *c*, the noun *church* refers to a congregation.

Since at present many mission efforts are winning only a few non-Christian men and women to believe on Jesus Christ and become responsible members of His Church, costly decisions will be required from churches, executives, and missionaries. Since the changes needed to make contemporary "good works" multiply practicing Christians and Spirit-filled churches in accordance with God's will, momentous decisions will be required.

Long-established programs of action, new theories of mission, and strongly held opinions as to what, under particular circumstances, the Bible requires are constantly debated. Mission associations swing away from what they have been doing to what they think they ought to do in the eighties and nineties. Prophets arise who stridently proclaim, "Path 1 is wrong. We must follow path 2." Other prophets demand that Christians follow path 1.

Shall we evangelize men and women of non-Christian nation-states? These people have their own lifestyles, religions, and cultures. Is it right, indeed is it Christian, to persuade them to follow ours? What is God's will in regard to these thorny questions? What does the Supreme Authority, obeyed by all Christians, say? The new world coming into being raises many such theological and biblical questions. The relationship between social action and evangelism and the proportion of missionary resources devoted to each is also a matter of great concern. The first nine chapters of this book are devoted to examining these questions. The answers given will lead the hundred thousand missionaries and their senders in very different directions. We must go only in the directions pleasing to God.

Those whose mind-set toward mission is still based on conciliar thinking from the 1960s and 1970s may, I fear, demur. But those whose thinking is geared to what the World Council of Churches said at Vancouver in 1983 will, I hope, welcome my findings. Similarly, evangelical leaders dedicated to mission as it has been may be troubled by this volume. But those seeking to adjust their thinking to this contemporary, radically changing world will, I believe, welcome it.

The rights of sending and receiving Churches often clash. In the colonial era western Churches propagating the gospel carried out their own convictions. In the era of self-governing nations, third-world Churches consider themselves the only authority. Has "mission," therefore, become "aid to young Churches"? Or is it still evangelizing the multitudes of unreached peoples (classes, tribes, castes) in all six continents where there is a small or often no Church? Ought a denomination of four hundred thousand members of the Kamba tribe in Kenya to tell its fathering mission from America where to evangelize in Tanzania and Uganda? Should a mission, which has in fifty years established a small cluster of congregations, in which are three thousand souls, withdraw all its missionaries and bring them home? Or should it send them on to the many surrounding *unreached* people? Who decides what the mission ought to do—the young denomination or the mission? The missionaries or the ministers? Such questions are numerous. So are the momentous answers given.

In the past, world evangelization has been thought of in relation to nation-states. Sending Churches carried out the Great Commission in Brazil, Indonesia, or some other nation. It is becoming clearer every day that every nation-state is made up of scores and sometimes thousands of separate pieces. The world is a beautiful mosaic of segments of society. Several chapters in this book are devoted to the fascinating intricacies of this important fact. As senders, executives, and missionaries begin to see the pieces of the mosaic clearly and discover which are responsive to the gospel and which are indifferent or hostile, they can determine the amount and kind of work needed in each piece for which they have assumed responsibility. Shifting from evangelism and church multiplying in a nation-state to doing these two essential tasks in specific segments of the population will not be easy. It will often be painful. But it is essential if the laborers are to hear their Lord say, "Well done, good and faithful servant."

During the past two hundred years the main questions facing Christian missions were how to get there and how to evangelize; but these are not the contemporary questions. Today in each of the multitudinous groups of unreached people, what the main task is and how to carry it out in an effective way are the essential questions. Dozens of other problems also demand solution. Momentous decisions have to be taken at every turn.

This book sets forth momentous questions which must be asked and momentous decisions which must be made. We shall discuss

1. Theological decisions
2. Decisions about the ethnic mosaic
3. Decisions about missionary societies
4. Strategic decisions

All thinking, teaching, and writing about mission should press on to actual discipling, to multiplying self-perpetuating congregations. Mission is not discussing ideas in classrooms or constructing reasonable theories. Mission is carrying out God's unswerving purpose. Mission is "blood, toil, tears, and sweat." Battles are won not at West Point but on battlefields.

The conciliar churches at Vancouver in 1983 heard many addresses about evangelism and passed many resolutions calling for evangelism. This is an excellent beginning. But unless substantial resources of men and money are now poured into evangelizing the three billion who have yet to believe, history may regard Vancouver as mere words. Conciliar churches have switched so thoroughly to mission as working for peace, building a new social order, outlawing thermonuclear war, granting women equal rights, and other good causes that they will find it difficult to return to eliminating the greatest poverty of all—that of not knowing and following Jesus Christ our Lord. Vancouver must be followed by momentous decisions at many board headquarters and by pouring millions in money and thousands in men and women into reaching the unreached in all continents.

In particular, the erroneous doctrine that mission is every church evangelizing in its neighborhood must be seen to be a very partial truth. Of course, every church should evangelize in its neighborhood, but so many younger churches have millions in their neighborhood that it is quite impossible for them to evangelize adequately. Missionaries must continue to be sent by all churches, younger as well as older, eastern as well as western, southern as well as northern. Only so will the three billion, rapidly becoming four billion, hear the Good News.

To be sure, it is prudent to see problems clearly and devise plans of action of which God will approve and which ought to work; but unless these preliminary steps are followed by momentous decisions, mission is not carried out. This book calls to decisive action.

Part **1**

Momentous Theological Decisions

God's Total Purpose and World Evangelization

David Howard, architect of the world gathering at Pattaya, says, "There is no doubt a need for Christians to view the *whole* world and *all* its issues, and ask, What should Christians be doing in view of the total situation?"

The Lausanne Covenant declares that the evangelistic task "requires the whole church to take the whole gospel to the whole world."

Pope John Paul II also speaks to the total situation. The World Council of Churches at its assemblies studies the whole world. Evangelicals also are saying, "What do we do in view of global conditions?"

Four Major Tasks That Concern Christians

The world is made up of many parts. Christians are properly concerned with every one. A holistic view of the world and of God's purpose is necessarily what everyone should take. They must work at all the tasks God assigns to them. Christians are necessarily concerned with at least four great tasks.

1. *The Church must evangelize all those—in families, neighborhoods, cities, states, and continents—who have yet to believe.* The three billion, rapidly becoming four billion, must hear the gospel. *Panta ta*

ethnē[1] must be discipled. World evangelization is "the greatest and holiest work of the Church," as Vatican II affirmed.

2. *Congregations in all denominations are composed of men and women who worship God.* The Church is a worshiping community. Christians are constantly at prayer. Congregations have stated periods of worship and encourage all their members to engage in daily personal and family devotions. God's total purpose necessarily includes leading all Christians everywhere to worship Him. Making provision for adoration, praise, confession, thanksgiving, and petition is an essential part of the total task.

3. *The Church must provide for systematic teaching of the Bible and systematic study of the Bible in homes, schools, churches, Bible schools, and seminaries.* Bible study does not happen accidentally. The Church must plan it, pay for it, and see that it occurs. A substantial portion of church resources must be devoted to carrying out this purpose of God.

4. *The Church must apply biblical ethical standards to all of life which it influences—families, neighborhoods, cities, states, and international associations.* Peaceful, merciful, and just nations and world are the goal that will be fully achieved only after Christ's return. Before that it is clearly God's will that as many just, merciful, and peaceful national and global social orders as possible be achieved.

Delineating the Tasks

All four major tasks and some others must be done. The Church is properly engaged in the expansion of knowledge, the creation of beauty, and the advancement of science. But for the time being we focus simply on the four great tasks mentioned. There is abundant biblical authority for each of them. On this point there can be no debate. For each task there must be a specialized task force whose

---

1. In all thinking about mission, it is essential that we understand the words *panta ta ethnē*. Romans 16:26 says, "According to the commandment of the eternal God, [the gospel] has been made known to all the nations (*panta ta ethnē*), leading to obedience of faith." *Ethnē* cannot mean "nation-states." Clearly the meaning is that the gospel has to be made known to all the peoples—tribes, castes, economic and social classes, segments of society—to lead them to the obedience of faith. Tens of thousands of such people groups are found in the world. It is God's unswerving purpose that these should be discipled—that is, enrolled in Christ's Body, the Church.

business is to do that particular work. We must care for the widows of the Greek-speaking Jews but must not neglect the preaching of the Word. Let deacons do their work and apostles do theirs. There must be and are four task forces, one for each of the following tasks:

1. Evangelizing the world
2. Worshiping God
3. Translating, expounding, and teaching the Bible
4. Applying biblical truth, so that God's will may be done on earth as it is in heaven

When the force devoted to task 1 sets about its work, it must not imagine that its real duty is to carry out task 2 or 3. When those assigned to task 4 assemble, they must work single-mindedly at task 4. Task force 1 must not substitute teaching the Bible to Christians or Christianizing the social order for world evangelization.

Obviously, as each task force carries out its own work it both influences and works at the other three. Fervent worship of God, opening the worshipers' hearts and minds to the Triune God, will certainly further Christian education, foster a more Christian social order, and win more and more adherents to Christ. Effective evangelism multiplies ongoing churches among unreached peoples. Missionaries lead converts to worship God; through mission schools, literature, and other ways teach them His Word; and thus extend ethical structures and actions into more and more pieces of the mosaic of mankind. Christians rejoice in this, yet avoid the confusion and error of imagining that seeing the total task means denying or neglecting its specific parts.

In short, each specialized force will see God's total purpose and *in its own way* emphasize it. Those who lead worship will sing,

> Mine eyes have seen the glory of the coming of the Lord;
> He is trampling out the vintage where the grapes of wrath are
>   stored;
> He hath loosed the fateful lightning of His terrible, swift sword;
>   His truth is marching on.

Christian educators who are teaching the Bible will emphasize sin, salvation, righteousness, peace, adoration, and evangelism. Those working at world evangelization will multiply self-propagating

churches in which worship, justice, brotherhood, and biblical instruction will certainly be emphasized.

All this has been done, is being done, and will be done. At the same
time each force will understand that it has its own special task.
Seminary professors will teach the winning and enrolling of *panta ta
ethnē*, but will not neglect teaching and rush off to evangelize a
receptive tribe in Timbuktu. Similarly missionaries will urge new
Christians to ethical action in their families, neighborhoods, and
cities, but will not neglect evangelism in order to engage in political or
military action needed to institute a more just and brotherly social
order.

As leaders of world evangelization plan future action, in view of
God's total purpose and their own special task, they will have to make
many momentous decisions. These will fit the state of church growth
in the particular segments of mankind with which they work, and
hence will differ from segment to segment. However, all decisions
ought to intend effective evangelism. When missions found schools
and hospitals, their chief goal must not be to contribute the best in
education and health to sister nations nor to uplift sections of the
global village. Missions maintain schools and hospitals in order to
advance world evangelization. A missionary society ought not to say,
"We are here simply helping this developing nation. Whether its
citizens become Christian or not is of no concern to us. The days of
world evangelization are over. Each religion will reconstruct itself,
borrowing whatever it chooses from Christianity and other religions."

Distinguishing the Task Forces

A major part of God's total purpose is making the gospel known to
all peoples so as to lead them to faith in Jesus Christ and obedience to
Him. In all mission planning and all distribution of budget and
manpower, therefore, that particular chief purpose ought to be
implemented. A certain amount of overlap no doubt will occur and
has occurred. In India, for example, the national revolt against
untouchability was certainly caused by the spread of Christianity; but
Christian mission did not go to India to attack and try to end the caste
system. The purpose of Christian mission is not to bring about peace,
mercy, and justice (1 John 3:1). It is to lead God's lost sons and
daughters back to Him. Then the former will follow.

It is a nice theological question whether Christians ought to spend
prayer, time, and money in working to bring in a righteous social

order among non-Christians—men and women of the world. We see no example of this in the Bible. Yet, because our Lord taught us to pray that God's will be done on earth as it is in heaven, and because Christians have constant contact with people of the world, it seems reasonable to hold that where Christians have political power, they should work to make the social order more ethical even if it is controlled by non-Christians. Today it is generally assumed that Christians ought to work for peace, justice, and compassion everywhere.

Consequently, just as the Church has a task force to carry out world evangelization (Mark 16:15), it ought to have a task force to work toward a righteous social order. Its marching orders would be the second sentence of the Lord's Prayer. It would recruit a task force and build organizations (e.g., abolitionist and prohibition societies) dedicated to rooting out evil structures in all ethnic units at home and abroad. These societies would address themselves not to worship, Christian education, and evangelism, but to effective political action. They would teach brotherhood and peace in all parts of Planet Earth. They would expose racism in all populations, whether these were Secularist, Marxist, Hindu, Muslim, or Christian. They would plead for more just laws. They would be the voice of the poor and oppressed in all nations. Oppressors and exploiters—from the propertied classes, the educated elite, or the common people—would fear this army of the righteous God.

To build a task force devoted to increasing righteousness in all homogeneous units, those now emphasizing social action will have to make momentous decisions. J. H. Oldham made such decisions when in the twenties he withdrew from the International Missionary Council to form the Life and Work Movement. The first three task forces, recognizing that God's total purpose is larger than the specialized work entrusted to them, will welcome the fourth task force. All Christians whom God calls to special tasks will press ahead obeying God, doing their own particular task.

Today, in view of God's total purpose, all Christians must ask three momentous theological questions:

1. Does God call Christians to make the gospel known to all peoples in all six continents in order to lead them to obedient faith in Christ?
2. In view of the total biblical revelation, how much attention ought

those whom God calls to this specialized task pay to other parts of God's total purpose?

3. Does God's total purpose require all Christians to work hard at everything? Is specialization unchristian?

Momentous theological decisions in world evangelization are never those which move mission resources into the fields of worship, education, or social action. They are always those which further making the gospel known to all peoples with the unswerving purpose of leading them to faith and obedience.

God's total purpose must be carried out; but everyone must not do everything. Carrying on God's total purpose necessitates providing a distinct task force for each great task. These specialized task forces must be recruited, trained, funded, and kept at work. While each will see and honor God's total purpose, each ought to do its own work. Only then will God's total purpose be efficiently carried out.

Today all of these contemporary considerations make it necessary to ask the following questions: Is carrying out "God's total purpose" Christian mission? Are missionary societies organized to carry out all aspects of God's holy will? In short, under the banner of "holism," ought missionary societies to turn from the universally accepted meaning of "mission"—that is, world evangelization—to doing everything God desires done?

The Meaning of the Word *Mission*

Today the word *mission* is used in three main ways. First, there are those who by "mission" mean the construction of a new, just, equitable social order. This was the meaning assigned to "mission" by the World Council of Churches (WCC) in its 1968 meeting in Uppsala. That the council took this stand is clearly seen by the fact that it almost totally eliminated references to world evangelization in its official pronouncements. The following passage from the preparatory papers also clearly indicates that the meeting was planned to turn mission from Christianization to humanization:

We have lifted up humanization as the goal of mission because we believe that more than others it communicates in our period of history the meaning of the messianic goal. In another time the goal of God's redemptive work might best have been described in terms of man turning towards God. . . . The fundamental question was that of the true God, and the church responded to that question by pointing to him. It was assuming that the purpose of mission was Christianization, bringing man to God through Christ and his church.[2]

Those who lift up humanization as the goal of mission are still fairly numerous. The WCC at Vancouver in 1983 did, of course, emphasize evangelism. Nevertheless, as one reads the assembly's findings, he has the uneasy conviction that the WCC still holds that the goal today should be humanization and that it has stressed evangelization only because of the great unhappiness expressed by evangelicals. An example of this is found in *Mission and Evangelism: An Ecumenical Affirmation*. It maintains that the "good news of the kingdom is a challenge to the structures of society, . . . as well as a call to individuals to repent."[3]

There is no question that the Christian seeks to live a righteous life, do justly, love mercy, and walk humbly with God. However, this is not evangelism! The good news that through faith in Jesus Christ one's sins are forgiven and eternal life is received is the gospel. The gospel is not a call to non-Christians and unbelievers to change social structures. Once men and women have believed on Christ and been saved, once they have heard and accepted the Good News, once they have become responsible members of Christ's body, the church, they are, of course, to be instructed in what the Bible teaches us concerning God's command for all of life. They are indeed then to practice goodness, peace, and righteousness. The insistence of the WCC that obeying everything which Christ has commanded is a part of the proclamation of the Good News is what must be rejected. Evangelism is one thing; good social action done by Christians is a different thing. They must not be confused. There must be task forces to do each.

The real position will be seen not in pronouncements at assemblies but in the allocation of men and money. When conciliar churches allocate as many resources to Christianization as they do to humanization, we shall all rejoice. Until then we must hold that the conciliar leaders are still counted in those who define mission in this first way.

Second, there are those who hold that the goal of mission is to carry

2. *Drafts for Sections*, prepared for the Fourth Assembly of the World Council of Churches, Uppsala, 1968 (Geneva: World Council of Churches), p. 34.

3. "The Gospel to All Realms of Life," *Mission and Evangelism: An Ecumenical Affirmation* (Geneva: World Council of Churches, 1983), p. 28.

out all phases of God's total purpose. Missions plant and manage large educational systems with multitudes of primary schools, middle and high schools, colleges, and seminaries. Missions carry out a tremendous program of marvelous and effective medicine that heals multitudes of men and women. Missions work to end evils ranging from cannibalism to the oppression of the poor, racism (castism), the tyranny of strong drink, infanticide, the low position of women, and so on. And of course missions proclaim Jesus Christ as God and Savior and persuade men and women to believe on Him and become responsible members of His Church.

Those who use the word *mission* in this second sense are also numerous. As we have already indicated, missions do carry on all these and many other works. Missions found churches, and the Church of the living God unquestionably benefits the lives of all its members, their institutions, customs, and every aspect of their being in many ways. Those who use the word *mission* in this second sense, however, studiously avoid any pronouncement as to what is the dominant purpose of mission and content themselves with the obvious fact that missions do carry on many different works. If asked about the dominant purpose of mission, they reply, "That depends on the circumstances. Under some circumstances it may be Christianization. Under some circumstances it may be humanization, and under still other circumstances it may be the building of beautiful cathedrals."

Third, there are those who define mission as all those activities whose dominant purpose is world evangelization. These persons consider that Christian mission means letting men know of God's plan for the salvation of the world and urging them to accept it. Although this is the dominant purpose, the third group of thinkers is quick to point out that mission carries on many different kinds of work. Under some circumstances—for example, among a largely illiterate population in Zaire—the work of mission, to which more than 50 percent of all resources were devoted for more than fifty years, was establishing a vast well-run system of schools. But even while the schools were being established and maintained and given more than 50 percent of the budget, every missionary concerned would have declared that the dominant purpose was the evangelization—the Christianization—of Zaire.

In a similar way when the great Benjamin Clough, in the midst of a great famine in India, used all his resources and very considerable government grants to build a huge irrigation system and employ and feed tens of thousands of starving people, he never lost sight of his dominant purpose, which was to lead these people to Christ. He wisely baptized no one during the famine (which lasted three years), but in the years immediately following the famine and this great work of mercy, the Baptist Church around Ongole grew to tens of thousands of members.

Note that those who use the term *mission* in this third sense readily acknowledge that as mission proceeds, it necessarily leads Christians in worship, encourages the formation of a glorious hymnology, builds beautiful churches, establishes systems of Christian education, teaches the Bible, fights and where possible roots out social evils and replaces them with more humane social structures. And it engages in much direct evangelization. But in all this it steadily maintains that its dominant purpose is world evangelization. It believes that only after men and women have come to acknowledge Jesus Christ as Lord and Savior and the Bible as their infallible and authoritative book are these other parts of God's total purpose effectively carried out.

This book uses the word *mission* in the third sense. I believe that this is the clearest use and the one best justified by biblical authority.

Also, those who use the word *mission* in the second sense will face the situations described and will be called on to make the same momentous decisions. I trust, therefore, that no reader will be so concerned with how mission is defined that he turns from a consideration of the enormous opportunities and dangers of the next two decades. This book has been written to highlight these and to urge that these costly decisions be made wisely and boldly in the light of realities.

2

The Theological Heart
of Today's Crisis

Basic to the conciliar drive to replace evangelism as the heart of Christian mission with action to rectify the injustices of the world and to usher in a Christian social order is a systematic downplaying of the Great Commission.

The Authenticity and Importance of the Great Commission

Liberals believe that many books of the Bible are made up of various strands which the final editor wove into one narrative. They operate on the assumption that the Great Commission was not really spoken by the risen Jesus on a mountain in Galilee and need not be understood as God's command. The final editor of the Gospel of Matthew attributed it to Jesus, perhaps as late as A.D. 100 or 120, to explain the remarkable spread of the Church in the Roman Empire.

For example, Lesslie Newbigin writes:

Since the time of William Carey it has been customary to take the closing verses of Matthew's Gospel as the fundamental mandate for mission. This text has often been referred to as the "Great Commission," and missionary work has been understood essentially as obedience to the "last command" of Jesus. . . . But . . . this way of understanding the motive of missions is not that of the New Testament. The Great Commission is nowhere cited in the New Testament as the basis of missions. At no point does any of the apostolic writers seek to lay upon the conscience of his readers the duty to evangelize as an act of obedience to the Lord. There is indeed an obligation involved, but it is never a matter of obedience to a command.[1]

Newbigin's interpretation of the Scriptures is questionable for two reasons. First, it is not what the biblical record says. Matthew 28:19 is not a lone verse. From beginning to end, the New Testament tells us of a universal Savior. He came to seek and save the lost, all those who do not believe on Him. His followers must do the same. John the Baptist, pointing to Jesus, said, "Behold, the Lamb of God who takes away the sin of the world." The word *world* is all the more significant because it was spoken to a Jewish audience.

John tells us that whoever—be he Chinese, African, Nordic, American, Indian, Japanese, or Turk—believes on God's only begotten Son will not perish but have everlasting life. Paul writes, "Whoever calls on the name of the Lord will be saved." Also, "God gave us eternal life, and this life is in his Son. He who has the Son has life; he who has not the Son has not life" (1 John 5:11–12, RSV). A universal Savior and a universal gospel—which to believe is salvation and which not to believe is eternal loss—places on every Christian a great obligation to tell others about the way of salvation.

"Yes, but," someone may say, "the Great Commission is nowhere quoted in the New Testament. Had it really been Christ's command, it would have been." Two errors stand out in this statement. First, the risen and reigning King says clearly, "All authority in heaven and on earth has been given to me; *therefore* going, disciple *panta ta ethnē.*" *Mathēteusate*, the Greek word for disciple or enroll, is an imperative, used only to command. Second, if anyone pleads that nowhere in the New Testament is the Great Commission "cited as a motive for mission," he must be reminded that nowhere in the New Testament is bringing in a peaceful, merciful, and righteous social order, God's reign on earth, cited as a motive for mission. What the New Testament tells us is that apostles and ordinary Christians, under the most trying circumstances, did tell others the Good News and did persuade them to become followers of Jesus Christ.

1. Lesslie Newbigin, "Cross-currents in Ecumenical and Evangelical Understandings of Mission," *International Bulletin of Missionary Research* 6 (October 1982): 146–47.

In Acts 8:4 we read that after Saul of Tarsus had burst like an avenging demon on the Christians in Jerusalem, they went everywhere preaching the gospel. Saul had had men beaten, women insulted, businesses ruined, houses burned; persecution had raged so fiercely that all ordinary Christians had fled from Jerusalem. *Then* these beaten, bloody, financially ruined Christians went everywhere preaching the Good News and persuading men and women in the villages of Judea and Galilee to believe on Yeshua Ha Maschiach, be baptized, and found churches of the living God. How could they do this without believing that the risen Lord had commanded it?

Some argue that apostles and ordinary Christians were impelled not by Christ's command but by an infilling of the Holy Spirit. No doubt the Holy Spirit had descended on the Church. The record is clear. But when the Holy Spirit filled them, why did they not gather for intensive prayer and study of the Scriptures and say nothing to anybody? Why was the infilling of the Spirit followed by ardent effective evangelism? Why was it not followed by attempts to better the Jewish social order? In a population expecting the Messiah to drive the Romans into the sea and establish an all-powerful Jewish state, why did not the descent of the Holy Spirit lead to the formation of fanatical bands of well-armed men preparing for the coming struggle? There can be only one answer to these questions. It is this.

Before Pentecost the Eleven had instructed the 120 that the risen Lord in Galilee (Matt. 28:16–20; John 21) had *commanded* them, "Disciple (*mathēteusate*) all peoples." The Greek word *mathēteuein* means to enroll in a school or to persuade to become a follower. That necessarily involves telling men and women about Jesus, whom God had made both Lord and Savior. This is exactly what the 120 did when the Holy Spirit came upon them. They rushed out into the streets and excitedly told everyone they met "Jesus whom you crucified, God has made both Lord and Messiah. He is alive. As He promised, He has given us the Holy Spirit. The Messiah will give the Holy Spirit to you too if you will believe on Him."

The coming of the Holy Spirit led to ardent excited evangelism because this is what the risen Lord in Galilee had emphatically commanded.

It is noteworthy that when his vast audience asked Peter and the rest of the apostles, "Brethren, what shall we do?" Peter included in his instructions these words, "Be baptized." Only in the earliest chapters of the Gospels do we read of those who would follow Jesus being baptized. Here, perhaps three years later, Peter tells all believers to "be baptized." Surely this was because only a few days earlier he had heard the risen Lord say, "Baptize them . . . and teach them to obey everything I have commanded you."

The great apostle Paul was also impelled by a command. He spent his life carrying out the Great Commission. He wasted no time calling inhabitants of the Roman Empire to form a new, just society in which punishment by crucifixion would be outlawed, the planned murders in Roman amphitheaters would cease, the institution of slavery would be ended, the position of women would be elevated, and free democratic government would be instituted everywhere.

In Romans, in a magnificent ascription of praise to God, Paul writes, "My gospel . . . according to the commandment of the eternal God, has been made known to all the nations, leading to obedience of faith" (16:25–26). What the Second Person of the Trinity had explicitly commanded, what the Third Person of the Trinity had driven Christians out to do, Paul here tells us eternal God had commanded. The good news was that on the cross Jesus Christ had borne the punishment of the sins of all mankind, and all inhabitants of Planet Earth could now be justified by faith in Christ. This was and is the gospel. The gospel is not the good social order which develops as Christians work to bring it in.

Paul devoted his life to obeying that command of eternal God. Romans 16:25–26 does not, of course, "cite" Matthew 28:19, because by A.D. 56 that Gospel in all probability had not been written and copies sent to all churches. But the passage in Romans does say exactly what Matthew 28:19 says—namely, that Christians are *commanded* to make the gospel known to all peoples with the purpose of bringing them to faith in Christ.

As the Great Commission is carried out, as multitudes in all segments of society become obedient Spirit-filled Christians, God's rule among them will spread. Not before. It is vain to expect that natural man, worshiping power, sex, money, and fame, will establish a just, peaceful, merciful society.

The Old Testament is full of exhortations to treat the poor justly, to alleviate their misery, to free slaves every seventh year, and so on. But these were the poor of God's own people. We nowhere read that Israelites were to have compassion on the Philistine poor, or the poor of the Moabites, Hittites, Assyrians, Babylonians, or Egyptians. The poor of Jericho were slaughtered with the rich. Paul's great concern for the poor in Jerusalem was not for the unbelieving Jewish poor, but for the poor among the Christians. This was not hardheartedness or a narrow racism. This was because until men and women have been born again, they cannot enter the kingdom of God. When men act from natural instinct, they are inevitably worshipers of self. They ask, "Will this benefit me?" They do ruthlessly what benefits them and their families, not what benefits others. This attitude is abundantly seen today. Even great cooperative movements such as the United Nations for the most part demonstrate that nations cooperate only as far as they see that such action will be good for them. They are not concerned with the welfare of others.

Feeding physically hungry non-Christian refugees today is beyond question a good thing to do, but it cannot be justified by the Old Testament exhortations to care for the poor or by Paul's raising money for the poor saints in Jerusalem.

The real reasons for downplaying the Great Commission and arguing that it is not a new law to be obeyed are two. First, as already stated, liberals do not believe that the Great Commission was spoken by the risen Lord in Galilee. Only by believing that the words were not spoken by the risen Lord can anyone maintain that in the New Testament Christians are nowhere commanded to proclaim the gospel and to disciple all the peoples of earth.

Second, under the whip of Marxism, with its goal of establishing a classless social order, many Christians of the affluent west have concluded that the supreme task today is not world evangelism but establishing a just society. They have then rushed to the Bible to justify the shift. We shall return to this second reason later on.

Harry R. Boer in *Pentecost and Missions* makes a good point—namely, that the Holy Spirit gave Christians power to tell everyone.[2] That is true. The biblical record is clear that He did. But that in no sense cancels the command. The Holy Spirit gave Christians power to do what Christ had emphatically commanded. The Holy Spirit also tells Christians how to carry out the command under particular circumstances. Paul, for example, tried to preach the gospel in Asia and Bithynia, and the Holy Spirit would not let him do so. Why did Paul want to disciple the peoples of Asia and Bithynia? He was impelled by Christ's command. But the Holy Spirit, in view of

2. Harry R. Boer, *Pentecost and Missions* (Grand Rapids: Eerdmans, 1961).

particular circumstances, possibly in view of the urgent work in Philippi, did not let him enter these lands.

Evangelicals are confident that each Christian, rejoicing in his salvation, full of new spiritual life, moved by compassion for the suffering and the lost, carries out Christ's command not as a burden to be borne, an onerous duty which has to be carried out, not as if his salvation depended on obeying this and other commands of Christ; but as a privilege. Evangelicals are also confident that as the Christian faces tomorrow, he sees clearly that, if this is to become a merciful and righteous world, nothing will better bring that into being than for all the peoples of the globe to become joyful, obedient, Spirit-filled followers of the Word of God incarnate.

But neither of these confidences wipes out the fact that He, to whom all authority in heaven and on earth has been given, commanded His followers to "disciple all the peoples."

We now go on to a third powerful version of the command. 1 Corinthians 10:33–11:1 reads, "I try to please everyone in all that I do . . . so they might be saved. Imitate me, then, just as I imitate Christ" (GNB). The phrase *imitate me* is in the imperative. In the New Testament the duty of evangelism, of telling all men the Good News, is laid directly on all Christians. As Paul did everything possible to bring men and women to saving faith in Christ, so must all Christians.

True, no Christian believes that those saved by grace and filled with the Holy Spirit obey this command as a means to their own salvation. That scarcely needs to be said.

A fourth and most impressive version, given in Romans 14:11 and Philippians 2:10–11, reads, "At the name of Jesus every knee should bow . . . and . . . every tongue should confess that Jesus Christ is Lord." This clearly means that the Great Commission in all its forms is God's command.

In view of this, Newbigin's statement that "the Great Commission is nowhere cited in the New Testament as the basis of missions" cannot be taken seriously. Certainly the Great Commission is not quoted word for word, but neither is any other command of Christ! Even more certainly the intent of the Great Commission permeates the entire New Testament. Unless the Great Commission is carried out, unless the eternal God's command (to make known the gospel to the end that all peoples everywhere shall believe) is obeyed, unless Christians and churches imitate Paul and Christ in being all things to all men that they may be saved, few knees will bow and few tongues will confess that Jesus Christ is Lord.

What about mission today? Distance has been annihilated. We reach the other side of the globe in hours. World travel is creating millions of men and women who think in terms of the global village. In this global village will Christian principles, revealed by God in the Bible, be accepted by all as the final rule, or will this be a secular state, in which men say, "Yes, of course, all religions have something good about them. They are all holy. But what is really true and practicable will have to be determined by *us*. We now know so much more than the writers of the Bhagavad Gita, the Analects of Confucius, the Koran, or the Bible."

If the Great Commission is authentic, if eternal God has commanded that the gospel of Christ be made known to all peoples with the intention of bringing them to faith and obedience, then Christians, while working to make this a Christian social order, will lay greater and greater stress on multiplying the number of individuals and *ethnē* who believe on Jesus Christ and accept the Bible as revealing God's will for mankind.

The authenticity of these commands is the central issue. If the Holy Bible is indeed God's Word, then the Great Commission in all its forms does, beyond question, lay on all Christians and churches the *command* to "disciple all the peoples of the world." That is the necessary step if the global village is to have an ethical social order pleasing to God.

The Great Commission and the Kingdom of God

This brings us to the topic of the kingdom of God, or the kingdom of heaven. The New Testament tells us that Jesus came preaching the kingdom of God. He sent out His disciples to tell all men that the kingdom of God is at hand. When they quote these passages, a substantial number of leaders of today's world Church say that when in a fluid society a new world order is being formed, the supreme task of all Christians, the mission of the church, must be to make sure that we make a just, peaceful, and righteous social order.

Here the essential question is, Is the kingdom of God simply a social order where all human behavior is soundly ethical? In other words, is the kingdom a society in which individuals may believe anything they wish about God, the universe, heaven, hell, sin, salvation, the gods and goddesses, and the powers, but must live according to ethical standards approved by all good men everywhere?

All considerations of the kingdom of God today must be clear on one point. The kingdom of God is not an earthly ethical social order, in which individuals may believe anything they like about God, Christ, and the Bible, as long as they act justly and peacefully. The Lord Jesus did not come preaching an ethical paradise, a human utopia. He came preaching a new social order in which He is King. He called on all men to believe on Him and be saved.

Another reason looms large for placing the top priority on effective evangelism, an evangelism which actually enrolls in the Body of Christ segment after segment of mankind.

This reason is that if God's rule is to be worldwide, if all knees in all the tens of thousands of *ethnē* are to bow, and if universal mercy, justice, and peace are to prevail, then it is essential that not merely a few individuals here and there but whole peoples (people groups, segments of society, economic and educational classes) be composed of Bible-believing, Bible-obeying, Spirit-filled Christians.

It would be childish to entertain the hope that natural man could possibly bring in the rule of God. Neither is it possible to believe that after sending us His Son to die on the cross for men's sins and after giving us His revelation in the Bible, God the Father Almighty would now say, "That was necessary two thousand years ago; but today what is necessary is a classless social order in which men give to each according to his need, and take from him according to his ability. Thus my rule among men will become operational."

If the Church of Jesus Christ wants to help bring in the rule of God, of which a Christian social order is a part, it must accept as axiomatic that a redeemed society is built of redeemed persons. Skyscrapers are built of steel, not mud. We rejoice in the small minorities of Christians now found in most countries of the still largely non-Christian world. In some lands Christians are numerous enough to influence law, national policy, and human relations. In those lands the secular body has a thin Christian backbone. But a much larger proportion of humanity must become practicing Christians before God's rule of righteousness, mercy, peace, and justice will prevail worldwide. As long as huge blocks of mankind are solidly non-Christian (whether Marxist, Muslim, Hindu, Buddhist, Secularist, or marginally Christian makes little difference), only limited degrees of peace and justice will prevail.

In the global village, Christ's followers will certainly try to treat everyone fairly, but Christians must abandon the naive thought that vast non-Christian populations will do the same. In order to establish "our rule," Josef Stalin killed twenty million, and just a few years ago in Cambodia, Pol Pot killed two million.

Christians are working day after day to transform their corporate living (whether on the family, neighborhood, city, state, or international level) into a form which God can bless. Whenever Christians pray, "Thy will be done on earth as it is in heaven," they are advancing such transformation. At one end of the spectrum transformation will be limited (as in the Amish Church) to a particular Christian community. At the other end, it will also enroll unbelievers in action which, being pleasing to God, will make laws, lifestyles, and other social structures more humane.

To be remembered is that the really Christian thing to do is not always clear. Some Christians think that in case of war strict pacifism is the only right position. Others, equally intelligent and devoted, believe that sometimes wars have to be fought. Assyrians and Moabites, Hitlers and Stalins have to be resisted. Some Christians believe that the death penalty is never justified. Others believe that it must, according to God's orders, be imposed for certain crimes. Christians in the United States are divided on whether abortion is sin or moral action.

This ambiguity has existed since the beginning. It is amplified today by the enormous number of nominal Christians and by the three billion who have no possibility of judging what is right and wrong by the Word of God. If a just, peaceful, and merciful society is to be born, we must rapidly multiply committed practicing Christians. This means enrolling men and women in Christ's school (*mathēteusate*) *and* teaching them "to observe all things He has commanded."

If we want world peace, carry out the Great Commission. If we want universal righteousness, carry out the Great Commission. If we want liberty and justice for all, *mathēteusate panta ta ethnē.*

Effective evangelism must be the highest priority in every Christian's life. With the threat of nongrowth menacing most congregations and most denominations, it is especially urgent that the Great Command be heard and obeyed. Far too many congregations are loving, caring groups of Christians which do not win from the yet-to-believe, the lost, a continuing stream of ardent believers.

In the United States, population 230 million, possibly 50 million are practicing Christians. In Great Britain, population 56 million, there may be 15 million intentional Christians. In Norway, with a population of 4 million, probably fewer than a million are committed Christians. In Brazil, population 120 million, there may be 20 million Bible-obeying Christians. Church attendance and participation in Communion are a good measure of the number of truly committed Christians. In "discipled" populations, every congregation ought to be obeying the command to evangelize which rings throughout the New Testament. Two tasks are involved: the evangelization of the 3 billion unreached men and women of the world, and the renewal of the 800 million nominal Christians. Increasing the number committed to Christ, who live according to the teachings of the Bible, is urgent.

With the threat of nongrowth, declining memberships, and sanctuaries which seat three hundred being occupied by fifty, the Great Commission must be heard again as a *command*. Downplaying the Great Commission must cease. Effective evangelism ought to become more common than telling the truth and being just to the poor. It is the only soil in which all ethical advance flourishes.

With the threat of thermonuclear war hanging over the globe and the likelihood that in the coming decades other ambitious men will seek to dominate the world just as the Kaiser did in 1914, Hitler did in 1939, and the Russians in these decades seem to be arming to do, we must rapidly multiply the number of practicing Christians. Christians should by effective evangelism transform each segment of society from within. This requires increasing the number of men and women who incarnate Christ's transforming power in every piece of the mosaic of mankind. We must expand the small minorities of practicing Christians in every body politic.

I write as one glad to have descended from abolitionist ancestors. In the mid-nineteenth century abolitionists worked to end slavery. This led the southern states, where four million blacks were held as slaves, to secede and try to form a republic in which owning slaves would forever be legal. Many of my ancestors died in the 1861–65 War to Free the Slaves. John Brown of Harper's Ferry was a hero in our family. I believe in Christian social action. It is a fruit of effective evangelism.

After men and women have been enrolled as Christians and baptized, they will be taught to observe all things Christ has commanded. Carrying out this never-ending process is one of Christ's many commands. Christian mission must not be defined as doing everything God wants done. Mission is not everything the Church does outside its four walls. Christian mission is enrolling in Christ's school as learners *panta ta ethnē* in every nation-state. This huge task is mission.

Those who are enrolled, who are crucified with Christ and can say, "It is no longer I who live, but Christ . . . in me" (Gal. 2:20), work ceaselessly for a more Christian (just, peaceful) social order. Social action is necessary. The relief of poverty, the lessening of pride in being educated, wealthy, and cultured, and the increase of general well-being are certainly good ends; but they must never be substituted for effective evangelism. It must never be thought that if we Christians, working with non-Christians, rectify the injustices which we and our nations have perpetrated, a sinless world order will emerge. That thought is a chimera inspired by Satan. God's rule will not descend on societies in which most men and women, scorning the lordship of Christ, intend to do what they think will benefit them.

It is in this kind of a world, with its lost men and women, that Christ commanded His followers to disciple all the peoples. It is in this kind of a world that God's command, so clearly enunciated in Romans 16:25–26, rings in the ears of all genuine Christians. It is in this kind of a world that Paul, using the imperative, says, "*Imitate me* as I imitate Christ" (italics added) in making every effort to bring souls to saving faith in Christ.

The Great Commission is a command. It is the biblical motive for Christian mission. In all six continents, as Christians, filled with the Holy Spirit, obey this command, we shall see communities transformed, counties rejuvenated, urban areas becoming cities of God, and whole nations marching upward to Zion. The world will be transformed into a place much closer to that which God will bring in on the great day when His will *will* "be done on earth as it is in heaven."

3

A Missionary Confession
of Faith

Like the New Testament, the Christian religion throbs with passion that men, through belief on Jesus Christ, be reconciled to God and become baptized members of His household. Written into all its books and almost all its chapters is the deep concern of God that men be saved—and salvation is defined as being called by and obedient to God and hence in right relationship to the Savior. From Him flow justice, peace, patience, brotherhood, goodness, self-control, and other fruits of the Spirit.

The Nature of a Creedal Statement about Mission

All creeds and confessions, if they would be fully Christian, should express the overriding intention of God that all men everywhere, in answer to God's choice of them, believe on Christ, repent, and live in Him. Every doctrine, if it is true to God's revelation in the Bible, should be colored with this dimension of God's will. Karl Barth saw this clearly, as his criticism of the traditional doctrine of the Church shows. The reformers held that the Church existed wherever the Word was rightly preached and the sacraments correctly administered. Barth agreed, but added that the Church is defined also by its marching orders. It has been sent to all the world to disciple, reconcile, and heal the *ethnē*—the thousands of peoples—of which

31

mankind is composed. Barth pointed out that the Church may preach the gospel correctly and celebrate Holy Communion faithfully every Sunday without ministering to the clamant and tragic needs of the non-Christian world. If the organism is the Church, he insisted, it must be concerned with the redemption of the world. It must carry out God's will for the world. Only then is it the Church.

This truth about the doctrine of the Church is being recognized today, but not applied widely enough. Grievous distortion of the doctrine of the Church results. Many examples from the statements of faith of many denominations could be given, but we shall focus on only two. The first will make the nature of a missionary confession of faith clear and will, I trust, emphasize that I am speaking to a disastrous lack in the creedal position of many denominations.

Emphasis on the Doctrine of the Holy Spirit

A statement of faith from a conservative denomination (not Presbyterian or Reformed) contains this typical article about the Holy Spirit:

> We believe in God the Holy Spirit, who came forth from the Father and the Son to convict the world of sin, righteousness, and judgment, and to regenerate, sanctify, and empower all who believe in Jesus Christ. We believe that the Holy Spirit indwells every believer in Christ and that He is an abiding helper, teacher, and guide.

This article is right in regard to the deity of the Holy Spirit. It is also right in respect to His proceeding ever from the Father and the Son—a timely emphasis today when Christians must know whether contemporary enthusiasms and labors are of God or not.

Is the Holy Spirit at work in all the good movements of our day? The Christians of the early church also asked this question. To answer it they formulated the creedal statement that the Holy Spirit proceeds ever from the Father *and the Son*. The *filioque* clause is no mere quibble of hairsplitting theologians. The problem the church fathers faced was that non-Christians spoke of spirits at work—from those of the fields and hearths to the philosophical configurations of the educated elite. "Our spirits," these non-Christians said, "are the Holy Spirit at work."

In the terse *filioque* clause the Church replied that God was, indeed, at work outside the Church, had of old spoken in "divers manners"

(Heb. 1:1, KJV), and was continually making Himself known to the eye of reason (Rom. 1:19–20). Furthermore, the Logos was certainly the light which enlightens every man (John 1:9). Nevertheless, the Triune God, speaking to men as the Holy Spirit, had also spoken to them as the Son, the Second Person of the Trinity. Therefore, He always spoke and acted in harmony with the recorded words and acts of Jesus of Nazareth. The Holy Spirit ever proceeds from the Father *and the Son*. All spirits, all inspiration, all claims that God is at work in current history, the forces of nature, or the spirits of the air must be tested by the simple question, Do these harmonize with God's Spirit manifested in Jesus of Nazareth? If they do not, they are not of the Holy Spirit.

The words *and the Son* in the creedal statement we are considering should be in all creeds written for the twentieth century. These words should be greatly emphasized, because today many Christian leaders do not admit or recognize that all values need to be checked against what the Son said and did. Man has no knowledge of the Son except what is recorded in the Bible. Not a chapter, not a sentence, not a word about Jesus Christ can be found in any contemporary writings of the ancient world. The Holy Spirit can operate outside the Church and can influence non-Christians; it is also true that there is only one way to determine whether a given value or a given course of action is of the Holy Spirit or not. That is to check the item in question against the record of what the Son said and did.

The debate about the Holy Spirit can be seen today in two very different areas. Many independent new denominations, which have been called nativistic movements, believe intensely that the Holy Spirit is at work in them. The Shakers on the Yakima Indian reservation in the state of Washington (not related in any way to the Shakers of Pennsylvania) maintain that they have the Spirit more than white churches and that He has for them an authority exceeding that of the Bible. In other words, this means that when they do what they feel is right, what Indian custom, economic conditions, state of education, and religious excitement move them to do, they are being led of the Spirit, and they submit to His leading whether this accords with the teaching of the Bible or not.

At the other end of the spectrum some Christians of the radical left maintain that God is at work in the revolutions of today. Among His servants are Castro, Mao, and Lenin. He who sent Cyrus of old and used the Assyrians for His purposes is at work today in the events of our time by destroying injustices and oppressions under which His people groan and by building a better social order. Obviously, Christians who believe that the Holy Spirit proceeds from the Father *and the Son* have something to say to both the Yakima Indian and Christians of the radical left.

As the Christian religion comes into closer contact with non-Christian faiths, the doctrine of the Holy Spirit proceeding from the Son will be greatly needed. The crucial question to ask of every innovation, every movement of men is this: Is this of man or of the Holy Spirit? If it is of the Holy Spirit, it will harmonize with the biblical record of the life and teaching of the Word made flesh.

On the deity of the Holy Spirit and on His relation to the Son, the article we are examining is right. Furthermore, it is right in regard to one of the functions that the Bible declares the Holy Spirit fulfills. He convicts of sin and He sanctifies believers.

But the article we are considering is entirely silent about the missionary passion of the Holy Spirit, concerning which the New Testament speaks so often—namely, that He thrusts the Church out to proclaim the gospel, prepares men of other religions and of none to believe on Christ, directs missionaries to some populations[1] and away from others,[2] and in general commands and coordinates the discipling of the ethnic units of mankind.

This silence is typical of most creeds. Most of them omit mention of the missionary passion of the Holy Spirit. Such omission is understandable. The Protestant creeds were drawn up in the centuries when Protestant Europe was cut off from the non-Christian world by Islam on the south and east and the Spanish and Portuguese navies on the west. Protestantism was busy reforming the Church rather than bringing the peoples of Asia, Africa, and Latin America to faith in the gospel and obedience to the Lord. For nearly three hundred years the Protestant Churches had practically no missionary conscience at all. No wonder their creeds are markedly deficient in this regard. No wonder there is still abundant room to reform the creeds to make them truer to the Bible and more adequate regarding mission.

Later, when missions were possible, creeds were revised by men vividly conscious of the need of the Church to be holy. They added to

---

1. "Sent out by the Holy Spirit, they . . . sailed to Cyprus" (Acts 13:4).
2. "They were trying to go into Bithynia, and the Spirit of Jesus did not permit them" (Acts 16:7).

the reformers' doctrine the unquestioned biblical fact that the Holy Spirit makes men holy. This rectifies part of the lack. Today we need to go the rest of the way and insert into the doctrine of the Holy Spirit strong, fully biblical clauses and sentences about the function of the Holy Spirit in bringing the multitudinous *ethnē* of earth to faith and obedience.

Emphasis on Evangelizing the World

The second example of a faulty confession of faith is taken from the famed Presbyterian Confession of 1967.[3] This illustrates the need of all communions to state and live by truly missionary confessions of faith, which are at the same time truly biblical.

I shall not comment on what was the chief storm center in regard to the Confession of 1967—namely, its position on the inspiration, infallibility, and authority of the Scriptures—but rather call attention to the following remarkable fact: that even the most severe critics of the Confession had little (or, in most cases, nothing) to say about its strange and truncated position on mission. The Confession of 1967 sets before us a well-prepared statement of faith, over which major battles were fought, on which major compromises were made, without rectifying or even recognizing its serious inadequacy as regards reconciling men and women of all tongues and tribes and peoples to God. If such an omission could occur in this notable confession of a great Church, it is likely to occur in others.

The Confession of 1967 recognizes that the Church must be about God's business. In trenchant paragraphs it calls the Church to face the evils of racial discrimination, poverty, social injustice, and war. It insists that in these tumultuous days, as God's people confess their faith, they must remind themselves and other Christians of the true nature of the Body of Christ, commit themselves to paths in which God wants His Church to walk, and dedicate themselves to the urgent contemporary duties to which He directs them.

All this is good. Yet the Confession remains incomplete. It omits or slights great sections of the need of the world. It bypasses great

3. All quotations are from *The Book of Confessions* (Philadelphia, the Office of the General Assembly of the United Presbyterian Church in the United States of America, 1966). In this book the Confession of 1967 is the ninth listed. References are listed by paragraphs. Thus 9.10 means the tenth paragraph of the Confession.

emphases of the Word of God. It thereby misrepresents God's will for today. It does not throb with passion that men through belief on Christ be reconciled to God. It includes long and detailed statements about social justice and brotherhood; it is tragically truncated on mission.

The word *mission* occurs frequently in the Confession of 1967 as, indeed, it does in a great deal of current churchly life in the west. But "mission" has come to mean "everything God wants done in the world" rather than "discipling the peoples" or "reconciling men to God-in-Christ." Thus, while the Confession of 1967 speaks far more about "mission" than any previous statement of faith, it speaks far less about the evangelization of the world than it ought. The term *mission* almost exclusively refers to good social action. Mission in the sense of bringing the three billion who have yet to believe into redemptive relationship to Jesus Christ is notable by its scarcity, one might almost say by its absence. Exactly this tendency is to be observed in many denominations and seminaries. They are speaking more and more about mission as social justice, and less and less about classical and biblical mission—that apostolic "sending" by the Holy Spirit to proclaim Christ and persuade men to become His disciples. The Confession of 1967 is an excellent illustration of a worldwide theological trend.

True, in regard to the article about Jesus Christ, the Confession states that "the risen Christ is the savior for all men" and "the judge of all men" and goes on to say:

> To receive life from the risen Lord is to have life eternal; to refuse life from him is to choose the death which is separation from God. All who put their trust in Christ face divine judgment without fear, for the judge is their redeemer (9.11).

But the implications of these statements for the unbelieving multitudes of all the continents and especially for those of lands where the Church comprises less than 1 percent of the population are notable by their absence.

The section about *the sin of man* nowhere states that his sin lies in wrong belief or the belief in idols and false gods, in manmade ideologies, in the worship of power, sex, and money, and in the rejection of the true light which lights every man. Despite Romans

1:21[4] and many similar passages, nothing in this section of the Confession of 1967 states that man's worship of his own good concepts and constructs is sin in God's sight.

The section about the Bible says nothing about the clear directives of the Bible concerning the proclamation of the gospel, but rather affirms that "as God has spoken his word in diverse cultural situations, the church is confident that he will continue to speak through the Scriptures in a changing world and in every form of human culture." This sentence (note its ten-word introductory clause) can mean that God will speak savingly to men through other cultures independent of the Bible.

If one examines the Confession section by section, one clearly sees that the main stress is not on communicating the Good News to those who have not heard it, but rather on reconciling man with man. One sentence reads, "To be reconciled to God is to be sent into the world as his reconciling community" (9.31), but goes on to say, "The church . . . shares his labor of healing the enmities which separate men from God and from each other" (9.31). In short, reconciliation is thought of as chiefly horizontal, man with man. Mission as communicating the gospel to others, enlisting them as Christ's baptized followers, and discipling the *ethnē* is not emphasized at all.

The Confession of 1967 assumes that men must get enough to eat, must be treated as brothers, and must live at peace. Exploitation and oppression must cease. On these issues it exhorts the Church to act, but it says little in regard to bringing men of all nations and religions to faith in the gospel. "My gospel," Paul tells us, ". . . according to the commandment of the eternal God, has been made known to all the nations, leading to obedience of faith" (Rom. 16:25–26).

The point is so important that I quote from the Confession of 1967 the entire section called "Revelation and Religion," which deals with the relation of Christians to non-Christian religions.

> The church in its mission encounters the religions of men and in that encounter becomes conscious of its own human character as a religion. God's revelation to Israel, expressed within Semitic culture, gave rise to the religion of the Hebrew people. God's revelation in Jesus Christ called

---

4. "Though they knew God, they have not glorified him as God nor given thanks to him; they have turned to futile speculations till their ignorant minds grew dark" (*Moffatt*).

forth the response of Jews and Greeks and came to expression within Judaism and Hellenism as the Christian religion. The Christian religion, as distinct from God's revelation of himself, has been shaped throughout its history by the cultural forms of its environment (9.41).

The Christian finds parallels between other religions and his own and must approach all religions with openness and respect. Repeatedly God has used the insight of non-Christians to challenge the church to renewal. But the reconciling word of the gospel is God's judgment upon all forms of religion, including the Christian. The gift of God in Christ is for all men. The church, therefore, is commissioned to carry the gospel to all men, whatever their religion may be and even when they profess none (9.42).

That last sentence is emasculated by the two preceding paragraphs in which Presbyterians confess that theirs is just one among many religions, has a human character, is culturally conditioned, and learns much from other religions. It is not clear why Presbyterians should tell others about this second-rate religion. The Confession, to be sure, says "the church is commissioned to carry the gospel to all men," but since the gospel is an integral part of the Christian religion and would not be known today but for the Christian religion (which, the Confession says, is one of many religions) why the church should bother other people with it is a mystery. The Confession would lead no one to think it is urgent for any Christian to "approach all religions."

This slight emphasis on Great Commission mission is all the more remarkable when it is contrasted with the tremendous emphasis on service and social justice. When it comes to serving the world, working "for every form of human well-being" (9.32), being sensitive to "all the sufferings of mankind" (9.32), meeting "the needs of the time" (9.36), and carrying out "daily action in the world" (9.37), the Confession becomes incandescent; its authors framed sentence after sentence and long paragraph after long paragraph.

The good men who drafted the Confession of 1967 were headed in the right direction. They were making a confession relevant to today's world. They were making sure that it thrust the Church into action against racial discrimination, war, and poverty. Why did they not speak against unbelief, wrong belief, idolatry, and the worship of self or power? Are not the three billion who have yet to believe grievously starved and unjustly deprived by their lack of faith in Christ? Are they not cheated out of abundant life here and eternal life hereafter? Do men suffer from lack of wheat Bread only? Is a famine of the Bread of Life no cause for pity?

The authors of the Confession wrote no paragraph, no sentence, no phrase cautioning Christians, as they battle racial discrimination, to be sure not to offend racists. They did not point out that the Church's convictions on justice and brotherhood have "been shaped throughout its history by the cultural forms of its environment" (although this is quite true). They did not suggest that in the war against apartheid, Christians should respectfully learn from the government of South Africa. They said nothing about the possibility that God is speaking to the Church through the caste system in India. Why then do they qualify the proclamation of the gospel in all these ways?

The Confession of 1967 illustrates that many churchmen, conservative as well as liberal, speaking to the real sufferings of the day, slight or omit entirely the most cruel suffering of all: that of the three billion who know nothing of Jesus Christ.

The Need to Revise Creedal Statements

Some Christian leaders, in alerting Christians to their local social duties, have diverted them from their global spiritual duties. They have emphasized duties toward man and minimized duties toward God. To rectify this grave deficiency, I am pleading that every confession of every Church and missionary society, conservative as well as liberal, should make sure that all doctrines throb with the passion of the New Testament. In these days when the worldwide spread of the Church (the discipling of the nations) is progressing better and faster than it ever has before, every doctrine must be revised to make sure that it is true to the revealed will and purpose of God in the light of the spiritual thirst and hunger of the three billion. Only then will it be adequate as concerns mission. The two examples that were discussed are ample indication that most current confessions of faith—even those framed by conservative Christians—do not correctly state the biblical position concerning the unwon multitudes of the world.

Christians do well to confess that just and brotherly conduct is mandatory for them today. In addition, they should revise every doctrine and article of faith until it proclaims that salvation through faith in Jesus Christ for all men in all nations, of all religions and of none, is the patent and unchanging desire of God. A few doctrinal statements will require considerable revision. Most, however, will need only slight changes. For example, a typical article about God in the creed of one notable Church states:

> There is but one living and true God, who is infinite in being and perfection . . . most loving, gracious, merciful . . . forgiving iniquity, transgression and sin . . . and withal most just and terrible in his judgments, hating all sin, and who will by no means clear the guilty.

This was adequate in 1600 when Christians were conscious only of "Christian" Europe—and China was farther away in time than the planet Venus is today. In today's world, however, any doctrine of God the Father Almighty must state His position on other religions. In this pluralistic world, it will not do to leave His will on this matter unmentioned. Theologians must guide the Church at this point. They must not take refuge in omissions, implications, and ambiguities. The article just cited would be made more biblical and more relevant by the addition of the following italicized sections:

> There is but one true and living God, *Father of all men of every tribe and tongue, ideology and religion, culture and civilization.* He is infinite in being and perfection, most loving, gracious, and merciful, forgiving iniquity, transgression and sin, *forbidding all worship of idols, self, and other gods,* and who will by no means clear the guilty.

Some men argue that all creeds are brief summaries of extended doctrines, made to be confessed, recited, or affirmed by Christians as an act of worship. Therefore they must be brief and aphoristic. Such men would say, for instance, that the confession *Christ died for us men* is sufficient. The pronoun *us* is to be understood inclusively and universally. As congregations confess this, they mean: "Christ died for us. We represent all men. When we say 'us men,' we are including all men of every land, race, and tongue. The four words imply the whole human race."

The flaw in this argument is that whenever creeds have been drawn up, the terse aphoristic form has sufficed for issues which have been settled and battles which have been won, but has never been deemed good enough for the crucial issues of the day. Thus, to counter Arianism, Athanasius and the Nicene Creed added to the seven words, "Jesus Christ his only Son our Lord," seven phrases aimed specifically at Arian errors—"very God of very God, begotten not made, being of one substance with the Father," and four others. In the creeds of the Reformation it is easy to recognize the phrases, clauses, sentences, and articles directed specifically against the errors of the medieval Church. Effectiveness in battle, not brevity, was the chief goal.

For example, the authors of the Confession of 1967 were not content with an aphoristic doctrine of the Church, out of which could be deduced that she is, of course, interested in brotherhood and social justice. The authors spelled out at great length the truth that God intends that all His children—the multitudes, the poor, the oppressed, victims of the social order, ethnic minorities, and conquered nations —be treated justly; that the social order itself in every land be transformed to make justice roll down like waters; and that Christ's Church have a similar intent.

A missionary confession of faith for today will in every doctrine similarly spell out at length the will of God, revealed in the Scriptures, that all men of every economic stratum, every tongue, every tribe, every religion, and every ideology be given the opportunity to accept Jesus Christ. Christians in whose heart God has placed concern for the three billion who have yet to believe will not be quieted by the argument that an aphoristic statement of the missionary bearings of each doctrine is sufficient. As Arianism, Romanism, intellectualism, and introversion have each in turn required makers of confessions and creeds to devote special attention to them, so now the very existence of the two-thirds of mankind (who live around the world and across the street from us and who know nothing of Jesus Christ) requires makers of confessions and theological systems to frame doctrines and articles which throb with the passion of Christ for the salvation of the peoples of the world.

The need for the Church to speak to all the pressing needs of mankind appears so reasonable and urgent that it is hard to understand how the ecumenical branch of the Church in its pronouncements of the past two decades has emphasized more and more exclusively physical and economic needs and has slighted, minimized, or ignored entirely the need to win men to Christ, reconcile them to God, and disciple the nations. It is also hard to understand how evangelical Churches have until recently played down social action and played up only the need for a radical change of heart, belief on Christ, conversion, and a vast discipling of the nations.

The deeply Christian and eminently reasonable course of action is to face the real world and *all* its suffering and to plead with men to accept God's plan for its relief. The Church, loyal to its Commander and Lord, has no need to fear the entrenched social systems and vested interests which hold so many men and societies in poverty and ignorance. Neither need it fear the ideologies, idolatries, and religions whose false and inadequate concepts and teachings continually lead men astray and prevent them from accepting Jesus Christ as Lord and Savior.

One wonders whether the ecumenical branch or the evangelical branch of the Church will be the first boldly to espouse a thoroughly Christian position on both fronts at once. What a day it will be when, instead of the truncated programs from the left and the right, one branch of the Church or the other (or both) will draw up statements of faith which take with utmost seriousness the primary need of men for radical rebirth through faith in Christ *and* their secondary need for just and equitable treatment here on earth. The theological position of some in the ecumenical camp may prevent them from framing effective and biblical dogmas in regard to the conversion of men, the discipling of *panta ta ethnē*, and the multiplication of Christ's churches. But many in the ecumenical camp and all in the evangelical camp have no such impediment. They should act at once to frame confessions which speak clearly and at length of God's will for the generation living in this world but called to be raised with Christ and live eternally.

What a glorious day it will be when missionary statements of faith, utterly true to the Bible and utterly relevant to the spiritual and temporal agonies of the world, are daily confessed by hundreds of millions of His disciples. Such confessions will encourage them, under the guidance of the Holy Spirit, to powerful action toward the redemption of the world! How much of this may be done before the Lord comes, no man knows; but this is certain: while He tarries, the duty of the Christian is to do His will.

4

Spontaneous Evangelism
and Church Growth

A romantic view of evangelism is abroad in the Christian world. It is often used to defend evangelism against the charge that it is aggressive and meddlesome. Sometimes it becomes a rationalization for no growth. Its advocates argue that a Church which does not have this unplanned spontaneous evangelism will not grow and, indeed, *should* not grow!

The Romantic View of Evangelism

The romantic view will express itself in language such as the following: The Christian is one who has been seized by a personal love coming from outside himself. He has been surprised by joy. He has been possessed by Christ. He has become a new person and sees the world in brighter colors. He walks lightly. The world to him is fresh and new. Love fills him and overflows from him. He fairly dances with irrepressible happiness. And he wants other people to know of the Source of his radiance.

His faith ignites faith in others. They say, "What you have I want." They light their candles at his fire. Around him form groups of believers in Jesus Christ. New communities arise and bless and reform the old communities in which they take shape. The new believers, quite spontaneously, show forth a quality of life which attracts. No one hates them. They overflow with love. They are delightful people, and through them the gospel spreads and spreads and spreads. They live within their ancestral culture as the first Christians lived within Judaism—going to the temple and observing the feasts and holy days—and yet gradually transforming the old system. There is no imperialism, no trampling on indigenous cultures. But the Christians, in the midst of rapidly changing customs and patterns, incarnate a new way of life so reasonable, sweet, and in tune with the times that men and women are drawn to it.

Christians filled with love offer men the opportunity to experience alternative patterns of individual and corporate life. This is true evangelism. This is what it means to live constrained by love. Nothing is artificial, nothing is planned. There is no passion that others will become Christian, no influencing others to follow Christ, no calculation of rates of growth and strategies of evangelism.

Someone has written,

> The evangelist's main task is to trust to love and to connect where he can. It is the Christ lifted up in the patient and humble quiet of his heart who, in ways beyond his knowing, is most likely to draw others. As to *his* priority, there is no doubt. He has no need to assert it further. If we can live and act in such a spirit, then I believe great prospects open up before us.

A Response to the Romantic View

What does the missiologist say to this romantic view of evangelism? First, he rejoices that "Christ in the heart" is indeed a spring welling up to eternal life. The fruits of the Spirit are indeed love, peace, joy, and other virtues. We all have known those whose lives have been transformed, and we thank God for them. Their example is contagious in a wholly unplanned way. Spontaneous evangelism of this sort is sometimes seen, and we thank God for it. But no one can say that only those who manifest this kind of spontaneous overflowing love are true Christians.

Second, the missiologist will ask what the Christian should do who has not been blessed with those natural gifts and that overwhelming consciousness of God. He loved God. He obeys Christ. He, like Paul, is sure of his calling. And he hears his Master say, "Go, disciple the nations." The missiologist points out that if the spread of the gospel had depended on those surprised by joy, it would not have spread far. Paul planned his missionary journeys. His messages were not received with wonder and joy. He was much more often driven out of town. He aroused an active hatred wherever he went. Our Lord said, "They hate me. Do not be surprised if they hate you."

Third, with the enormous numbers of men and women who have not heard of the Lord of love in any adequate way, it seems the better part of wisdom to encourage Christians whose gifts do not include the attractiveness of Francis of Assisi nevertheless to bear witness, to proclaim Christ, to depend primarily not on their own charm, but on His grace and His power. After all, we proclaim not ourselves but Christ. Evangelism is proclaiming Him and persuading men to become His disciples and responsible members of His Church. We, the earthen vessels, point to the Treasure, not to ourselves. Evangelism is one who has found food, and is therefore no longer a beggar, telling still hungry beggars where to find food. Whether his is spontaneous telling, charming telling, a telling which excites no animosity and radiates love and light, or whether the vessel exudes a certain earthiness, a certain roughness, is really beside the point. He is not proclaiming himself. He is pointing to the gleaming Treasure in which is no blemish and which is worth so much that a man should sell all he has and seek to buy it for himself.

Spontaneous evangelism, as one kind of evangelism practiced by supersaints and filling all the rest of us mortals with joy as we behold it, is a very good thing. But when advocated as the only valid kind of evangelism, the chief kind of evangelism, or even the most effective kind of evangelism, it is dangerously close to being a sentimental, romantic structure whose real purpose is defensive. The argument runs as follows: Christians very seldom manifest anything like the totally love-filled life; therefore the less evangelism they do, the better. Unless they themselves are radiant transformed persons, no one will believe what they say about Christ. So let us have no evangelism until every Christian is a Francis of Assisi. The current lack of evangelism is exactly what *should* be seen in our Church. What we need is not evangelism but a tremendous purging and renewing of the Church until it becomes only those who are truly filled with Christ. Such Christians will multiply.

Paul, covered with bruises which he had received in the last town where he proclaimed the gospel, from those whose animosity it had excited, goes right on to the next town and proclaims it again. The record does not tell us that he debated with himself, saying, "Did I get beaten for the gospel's sake, or because I was unnecessarily blunt and maybe a bit sarcastic in presenting it? Is there any way I can be more charming, more irenic, more on the Hebrew wavelength? Would it not be better to sow the seed in peace and quiet than to try to take out of each synagogue those who believe and trust Yeshua Ha Maschiach? The seed in God's good time will bear fruit; the whole group, without ceasing to be Jews, while still excluding Gentiles, will peacefully become baptized followers of the Messiah. Let us trust to the quiet work of the Holy Spirit." On the contrary, the record says that, confident that the animosity had been generated by the claims of the gospel, the apostle went on to present it in very much the same way. It excited very much the same result. Those ordained to eternal life were baptized and gathered into a new church, while those who rejected the gospel were furious with Paul and assaulted him without mercy. "Woe is me if I preach not the gospel!" was his perpetual cry.

To sum up, the Christian advocate will, of course, be as tender and courteous as possible in presenting the gospel. He knows that the surest way to get the message rejected is to present it in an insensitive fashion. He could not be a responsible ambassador by being rude. The Christian advocate will always proclaim the Treasure, which is Christ, through his own imperfect personality, his hesitant speech, his poor grasp of the language of the receptors, and his inevitable bias. These imperfections will never become for him an excuse for no evangelism.

"Look at the Treasure," he will cry. "Don't look at the earthen vessel. You too in your own earthen vessel can have the gleaming Treasure. Go sell all you have and buy this Bread of Heaven."

This display of the Treasure is true evangelism. The utterly charming display is a rare special variety. Let us not sentimentally imagine that only those with the special grace can be true ambassadors; rather let us all, however gifted, faithfully proclaim the gospel to the best of our ability.

5

Evangelism and Preparatory Grace

Evangelism is not selling a product. It is discipling individuals and *ethnē*.

We tell the Good News. We bear witness that Jesus is the Christ. The Holy Spirit convicts men of sin, of righteousness, and of judgment. Men are "added to the Lord." God touches the hearts of people. God's grace saves men.

Nevertheless, the believer is expected to witness, proclaim, and live in ways that make the gospel intelligible and credible. It would be ridiculous for him to preach in Los Angeles to white, Anglo-Saxon, Protestant nominals in Hakka Chinese, or to the Maasai in Kenya in German. He must not only say the right words but also say them in linguistically and culturally acceptable ways. The more his life bears out his words, the more credible they become.

Furthermore, God continually broods over the human race, making some of its segments responsive. God takes human personality seriously. He has given men and women free will and respects it scrupulously. If they turn toward Him, He assists their turning. The Secularist, seeing it differently, says that as various forces—travel, industrialization, migration, military defeat, printing, radio, evangelization—play on mankind, some segments of society become ready for change. Strict Calvinists will describe receptivity to the gospel in still another way. Whatever the explanation, when the gospel is proclaimed by word and deed in an intelligent, credible fashion, some segments are much more likely to respond in faith than others. The Christian is commissioned by God as a faithful steward to speak to all, but especially to those in whom he discerns some preparatory grace, from whom he receives a welcome for the gospel, or who ask, "How may we be saved?" (Acts 16:30; cf. Matt. 10:14; Mark 6:11; Luke 10:10; Acts 13:51). To these he delivers a specific invitation to repent and believe on the Lord Jesus.

Thus Christians and missionaries should not be talking to everybody about everything. They should be devising specific communications to specific groups in which they discern a moving of the Holy Spirit. This is what they must do to be faithful stewards.

Our Lord spoke sternly to the multitudes, saying, "When you see a cloud rising in the west, immediately you say, 'A shower is coming'. . . . You hypocrites! You know how to analyze the appearance of earth and sky; but why do you not analyze this present time?" (Luke 12:54–56). He was referring clearly to their willful obtuseness regarding His coming. This is my point too. When He is coming to some segment of a population and turning it responsive, and finds few Christians harvesting there, will He not say to us, "You hypocrites! You know how to analyze the appearance of earth and sky, of sickness and health, of social unrest and revolution, of movements of the stock market, appreciation of your property, and the mysterious processes of inflation; but why do you not know how to interpret my coming to the multitudinous responsive segments of the human race?" The obedient steward, as a mark of his obedience, will discern where the finger of God is pointing. The alert servant, as a mark of his faithfulness, will observe when the Spirit moves the water of healing and rush to put the sick man in.

The following illustration of the need for devising specific communications to specific segments of the population must not be taken as in any sense presuming on the sovereignty of God. It does say something, however, about the obedience and common sense of the servant.

Tom Dillon, president of the advertising firm of Batten, Barton, Dustine and Osborn (BBDO), was quoted in the *Los Angeles Times* (Dec. 8, 1969):

The advertiser's primary aim is usually to get someone to make a purchase decision in his favor. But in most cases, the decision is made by a relatively small percentage of the population. For instance, about 80% of the beer is consumed by just 20% of the beer-drinking population. . . . A mere 14% of those who drink whisky buy 90% of the bourbon sold in the country. It's very expensive . . . to use ads to influence the decisions of people who are not the important decision-makers (or not really going to buy).

We spend a lot of time finding these prime prospects (the small but specific parts of the total population *who are likely to buy the product)* and then we try to learn what their problem (in regard to the product) is. After that, it's a matter of convincing them that we have a better solution to their problem. . . .

For example, the prime prospect for Philco color TV is a 37-year-old sports buff who still is not sold on the quality of color. The prime prospect for MJB Coffee is a 40-year-old California housewife who drinks five to eight cups a day. When Campbell Soup wanted to single out a market segment of light users that could be converted into heavy users, BBDO found the prime prospect to be a 29-year-old housewife with no children who worries over what to feed her husband (middle income, blue collar) when he comes home for lunch. Out of this came Campbell's "The Manhandlers" campaign for its thicker, richer soups. . . .

Once we (advertisers) talked to everybody about everything. Now we pinpoint the media and the creative content and talk to people with a specific frame of reference (in other words, we talk to specific people about a specific subject).

Specialists in selling deliver a meticulously stated message to a small but specific segment of a total population—a segment they have reason to believe is responsive to the product they are advertising.

Missionaries and missionary societies could with profit take this lesson to heart. The Christian who talks to everybody about the grace of God is likely to lead few to Christ. But the Christian who discerns those small segments of a total population which the Holy Spirit has turned responsive and who constructs a message about God's grace which is likely to appeal to those segments is likely to lead more lost sons and daughters back to their Father's house. God speaks through him precisely to those segments of society which He has turned responsive. When the Christian sees God's finger pointing at some people in Egypt and hears God saying, "Bring this people out of bondage into my glorious freedom," then the Christian had better learn the language of that particular people and construct a meticulously stated message suited to it.

As John Wesley surveyed the social scene in Britain, he made it his fixed purpose to proclaim the gospel to those segments of the population which were responsive to it. He discerned God's preparatory grace. He believed that the Holy Spirit, brooding on mankind, opened certain groups of men and women to God. Ever since then preparatory grace has been one of the doctrines emphasized by Methodists.

Momentous decisions hinge on recognition of God's preparatory grace. As missionary societies become conscious of the human mosaic and study its many pieces, this doctrine calls them to focus attention on those ready to hear. They have become ready to hear not by accident, not by some fortuitous circumstance, but by preparatory grace.

The obedient executive of a missionary society, intending to obey God in every detail, believes that the *ethnos* which welcomes the gospel is at the same time a directive from God saying, "Evangelize this ethnic unit, this economic or educational class." All obedient servants of Christ, once they recognize these instructions, will make momentous decisions to carry them out.

The doctrine of preparatory grace describes the actions of God which turn various segments of the human race toward faith in Christ. When the Holy Spirit inclines the mind of a non-Christian to accept Jesus Christ or to listen to the gospel with interest, then that man is experiencing preparatory grace. When God inclines many individuals in some one *ethnos* to listen hungrily to the gospel, that segment of mankind is experiencing the guidance of the Holy Spirit.

The sovereign Lord acts in sovereign ways. He is not bound by the ideas, wishes, or expectations of either Christians or non-Christians. Nevertheless, as we study His dealings with men during the past two thousand years, we discern oft-repeated patterns. We see that often certain portions of the population have by God's action been turned responsive. The doctrine of preparatory grace teaches today's Christians to look for such responsive segments and to focus on them adequate efforts. Those who engage in world evangelization should recognize that they serve a God who in these days in

sovereign fashion is turning whole segments of mankind responsive.

Those responsible for making decisions about world evangelization
can count on God's preparatory grace and should spend considerable
time and money discerning where it is operative, and then make
momentous decisions deploying adequate evangelistic resources there.
God commands Christians to reap the fields He has ripened.

6

Proclaiming and Discipling

What is the tension between preaching and discipling in world mission? The crucial theological issue concerned arises from two famous passages of Scripture. Mark 16:15 says, "Go into all the world and preach the gospel to all creation."[1] Matthew 28:19–20 says, "Go therefore and make disciples of all the nations, baptizing them in the name of the Father and the Son and the Holy Spirit, teaching them to observe all that I commanded you."

Each has many cognate passages, of which I mention two. Mark 16:15 is buttressed by Acts 1:8, "You shall be My witnesses both in Jerusalem, and in all Judea and Samaria, and even to the remotest part of the earth." Matthew 28:19–20 is buttressed by Romans 16:25–26, which in the New American Standard Bible reads: "My gospel . . . according to the commandment of the eternal God, has been made known to all the nations, leading to obedience of faith."

---

1. It is well known that the last twelve verses of Mark are not found in the oldest manuscripts. However, since down the past two centuries, Mark 16:15 has been a most influential verse in creating a missionary conscience in all denominations and since it voices a command repeatedly referred to throughout the New Testament, I use it without hesitation. I trust that readers will not allow textual questions to divert them from the unquestionable truth that the New Testament as a whole does speak to the entire world.

Note the difference between these passages. Mark and Acts say, Go, preach, and witness everywhere. Matthew and Romans say, Go, bring all *ethnē* to faith and obedience. Disciple them. Baptize them. These passages are put into sharp antagonism, one to the other, by the fact that some individuals and some nations are highly resistant to the gospel, whereas others are responsive.

Mission to the Receptive and to the Resistant

Note carefully this fact in the midst of which Christians, obeying their Lord, carry on world mission. Populations respond to the gospel unevenly. Seventy percent of the population of one district in India has become Christian; in most districts in India less than 1 percent has. Between 1898 and 1940 in two Korean provinces, North Ping Yang and South Ping Yang, the Presbyterian Church grew hugely. In the provinces around Seoul its growth was disappointing. In 1965 in Brazil the Methodists numbered about sixty thousand, the Pentecostals about a million and a half, and the Congregationalists only ten thousand. Congregational missionaries were speaking to *all* Brazilians, and these were resistant. Pentecostals were evangelizing the poor, and these welcomed their message. Spotty response marks mission. Some populations are resistant, others receptive.

Furthermore, almost all populations are resistant when they first hear the gospel. It comes to them in foreign costume with uncouth, irrelevant meanings. It is upside down, according to their culture. In most populations, therefore, as the Church carries out mission it must allow a period of years for the seed to be sown, germinate, and mature. Periods of germination look like periods of rejection. It is difficult to determine when the seed is growing unseen toward sure harvest, and when, because it has been carried away by the Evil One, there is no seed there at all.

I was speaking in the Tenth Presbyterian Church in Philadelphia twenty years ago, when Everett Koop, now surgeon general of the U. S., asked, "Why is it that though we are here on the edge of a large black district, full of people who need Christ, and are an integrated church and welcome blacks, only a few of the elite of black society have joined us? The people who need Christ most seem untouched by our ministry."

Some populations at home and abroad are resistant and some are responsive. Suppose a missionary is sent to a population that sets its face like flint against the gospel. What happens? He plants only one church made up of himself, his wife, his employed helpers, and a few dozen converts or orphans. After that he finds that no matter what he does, he can plant no more churches until he starts another mission station with another missionary family and other employed helpers. Facing such a resistant population, the missionary leans back on Mark 16:15 and Acts 1:8 as his authority and consolation. He is profoundly convinced that the Lord has called him to preach everywhere, be faithful, and leave the results strictly in the hands of God. "My task," he says to himself, "is to bear witness to Christ by word and deed, perhaps especially by kindly deed. I must tell the story of Jesus. That is my sole responsibility. And perhaps it is better to help people by deeds of kindness which people understand than to try and persuade them to receive Christ, which they mistake for religious imperialism."

Years ago Roger de Foucauld went as a missionary to North Africa. There, facing intense Muslim opposition to the name of Christ yet feeling compelled to witness to Christ, he formulated this theory and definition of mission: "Mission is a Christian simply being there, with a presence willed and determined as a witness to the love of God in Christ." In the sixties the Christian Presence series of books was published; the series built on this theory of mission, which arises in the face of intense resistance. It says, "We are not to disciple the nations, or bring them to faith or obedience. Only God can do that. We are simply to bear witness to Christ, by word or deed, and often by our simple presence." This view of missions results when a missionary goes to indifferent or resistant populations.

Suppose, however, a missionary is sent to a population from which, after a period of seed sowing and germination, thousands obey the gospel and walk down into the waters of baptism; many churches arise. What happens? This second missionary regards Matthew and Romans as his authority. He is profoundly convinced that God has called him to disciple *ethnos* after *ethnos*. He believes that "according to the commandment of the eternal God [the gospel] has been made known to all the nations, leading to obedience of faith."

Thus there have come to be two distinct varieties of missionaries. First there are those who go to peoples who reject the gospel—Hindus, Buddhists, Muslims, Marxists, and Secularists. These missionaries find their satisfaction and their fulfillment in obediently proclaiming Christ or quietly serving men in His name, distributing relief goods to needy humanity, educating the ignorant, or aiding in social action for just ends. One can enunciate a principle: when resistance is high, missionaries turn from proclaiming Christ to other good and Christian activities, which then become "mission." Second, there are missionaries who go to those who accept the gospel and plant dozens or hundreds of churches across a countryside. For them "mission" consists of multiplying churches and so educating and serving them that their members become more and more Christian.

These two types of mission must not be supposed to be rigidly separated. On the contrary, much overlapping occurs. Some missions to the resistant have a few missionaries working in a receptive pocket. Some missions to receptive populations encounter rebellious sections where only a few small churches arise and remain for decades.

Of the thirty-six thousand Protestant missionaries from North America, no one has counted how many are of the first and how many are of the second variety; but it would not surprise me if fewer than six thousand are engaged in multiplying churches and more than thirty thousand are either serving static denominations or carrying on mission work where over the years few become Christians. The thirty thousand lean hard on Mark 16:15 and Acts 1:8.

In delineating those two main kinds of Christian missions, I am engaging in no mere intellectual exercise. I am not classifying for the sake of classifying. That there are these two varieties of missions is a prominent theological characteristic of missions today and results in many a log jam. How each is to be conceived and the relations between them is one of the major theological issues in the missionary enterprise and will require momentous decisions.

What Is Biblically Justified?

Witness, the first variety of missionaries say, is the kind of mission the Bible requires. Certainly "witness" is an honorable word in the New Testament. However, since probably thirty thousand missionary lives from North America alone, untold treasure, and the main thrust of missions tomorrow are at stake, we cannot accept their conclusion lightly. We must search the Scriptures. Is their view of mission what the Bible really requires? In resistant populations does a true theology of mission send us in merely to be there, a Christian presence? Or at best to proclaim Christ, as our complete task? Conversely, do those who lean on Matthew and Romans lean rightly?

Is the proportion right? Do we have theological justification for thirty thousand missionaries welded to populations of scant church growth and six thousand to populations where churches multiply? Is this proportion justified by the Bible? Is this what God intends His faithful servants to do? In the receptive world of today, with the large resources we now have and the enormous resources Christians control, what is the proportion God would expect faithful stewards to put into operation?

Seed sowing is, of course, necessary. If no one sowed the seed, where would the harvest come from? Some missionaries should devote themselves to pioneer seed-sowing evangelism, but is the proportion thirty to six the right one? Is the exegesis on which it rests correct?

Exegetical Examination of the Passages

Theologians are accustomed to examining the Scriptures regarding doctrines such as the authority of the Bible, the sovereignty of God, the fall of man, the atoning death of the Savior, and the resurrection of Jesus Christ. It would seem normal that they should examine the crucial texts to see whether they demand proclamation to the resistant and discipling of the responsive as coequal ends. This is the doctrine in debate. Confusion here is the cause of many a deadlock. This is a crucial issue in missions tomorrow. In the brief examination of the text which follows, I shall argue that correct exegesis of the applicable passages will not support that doctrine.

An elementary principle of interpreting the Bible is that the meaning which the passage had for the writer and those to whom he wrote is the meaning first to be assigned to it. What meaning did Mark 16:15 and Acts 1:8 have for Luke, Mark, Theophilus, and other early Christians? What did Mark and Luke mean when they quoted our Lord's words, "Go into all the world and preach to all creation"?

These sayings of the Lord were penned in the years following the great battle with the Judaizers who resisted taking uncircumcised Gentiles into the Church, "speaking the word to no one except to Jews alone" (Acts 11:19), and hounded Paul to his death. It seems reasonable to assume that these sayings were written into the record to establish beyond doubt that it was the Lord's will that uncircumcised Gentiles everywhere could be and should be discipled, that as Acts 11:18 says, "God has granted to the Gentiles also the repentance that leads to life."

The issue in those early years was not preaching to those who rejected the gospel or discipling those who accepted the gospel. The issue was whether the gospel was to be shut up to the circumcised, descendants of Abraham according to the flesh. These passages say emphatically that the gospel is open to all men, and Christians are commanded to carry it to them.

Therefore, these passages by themselves throw no light on the great issue we are considering: Does God regard preaching to those who reject the gospel as of equal importance with discipling those who accept the gospel? The first two passages were never intended to command thirty thousand American missionaries to preach the Word where they cannot plant churches; the second two were not meant to command six thousand American missionaries to disciple responsive populations. To use the passages thus is not sound hermeneutics.

Is there then no light in the Bible on our problem? Rather there is much light. Our Lord directed His disciples as they spread the gospel to go to those who welcomed it enough to entertain messengers in their homes. Where the disciples found no welcome, they were to shake the dust from their feet as a testimony against the place and hurry on to those who would welcome them. This admonition, these marching orders, are found in the synoptic Gospels and Acts.

The early church practiced exactly these directions. Paul and Barnabas knew of them and acted on them. Acts 13:51 says, "They shook off the dust of their feet in protest against them and went on to Iconium." Notice the phrase *against them*. It is evidence of an exact knowledge of the Lord's words. He had referred to an ancient practice with roots in animistic religion. The dust shaken off was sacred earth. It would mingle with mother earth to which everything returns and remain there in that place to bear witness against those who had rejected the gospel. Man can be silenced, but not mother earth. When the early church used this saying of the Lord about twenty years after His ascension, she used it exactly. The dust was shaken off to bear witness against the resistant Jews of Antioch of Pisidia. They had heard but had not obeyed. Hence the messenger was to hurry on. Proclaiming the Word to those who rejected the gospel was not the task the Lord had assigned them.

Acts 13:46–47 is also vivid evidence that the early church did not lay siege to resistant populations or stay to serve them with schools or hospitals. To the resistant Jews in Antioch of Pisidia, Paul and Barnabas said, "Since you repudiate it [the Word of God], and judge yourselves unworthy of eternal life, behold, we are turning to the

Gentiles, *for thus the Lord has commanded us*" (italics added). It is difficult to avoid the conviction that this verse is not a chance remark of Barnabas but rather is a formula our Lord had voiced, the disciples had used in His lifetime, and the early church had learned by heart and spoken in thousands of villages to perhaps tens of thousands of families. This is particularly likely, since only four verses further on we read about Paul and Barnabas shaking off the dust against Pisidian Antioch's resisters.

However, we must not misapply Scripture. These passages speak to the small weak Church (A.D 30–100) that faced both those who accepted and those who rejected the gospel and was unable to reach both. In those particular circumstances the Bible does say to shake the dust off one's feet and hurry on to the receptive. These passages are not speaking to the enormously strong denominations (Churches) of today who seek God's will in regard to perhaps two billion resistant men for whom Christ died. What is God's will for us, facing our two billion resistant and perhaps half that number responsive?

The Practical Application of Scriptural Directives

We must go back to our Lord's sayings to go into all the world, preach to all creation, and disciple all peoples. We must study Romans 16:26, which may be a saying of our Lord not recorded in the Gospels: The gospel "now is manifested, and . . . according to the commandment of the eternal God, has been made known to all the nations, leading to obedience of faith." We must remember the word in Romans 5:18, "through one act of righteousness there resulted justification of life to all men." Our Lord intended that all should have a chance to believe and died to make that possible. Romans 10:13–15 is particularly instructive. The sending of the preacher is precisely in order that they may be saved. Romans 10:13 says, "Whoever will call upon the name of the Lord will be saved." The goal in Scripture is never proclamation for proclamation's sake. It is always proclamation that men may believe, repent, be baptized, and be "brought to the Lord" (Acts 11:24) in the Church of Jesus Christ.

Some argue on the basis of Romans 3:4 that much preaching to resistant peoples is properly done to justify the righteousness of God. They believe that since God is inevitably going to find men guilty of sin and thus condemn them, preaching of God's gracious way of salvation to all men is necessary so that they will be without excuse. They will not be able to plead ignorance of the way of salvation. Since the

righteousness of God, available to all who believe, has been manifested apart from the law, Christians should proclaim this available
goodness so that God may be justified when He punishes them. They
had a chance to repent and did not take it.

What shall we say to this argument? Far from buttressing proclamation for proclamation's sake, this strand of Scripture reinforces the
position that the basic purpose of proclaiming Christ is that men
believe and be saved and be added to the Church. The full argument is
that preaching about God's gracious way of salvation to all men is
necessary so that as many as possible will believe and be saved and
only those who stubbornly will not believe will be without excuse. God
is justified only if the way of salvation offered is a real option to all.
Thus the preacher must so present the gospel and so persuade and
encourage those who hear that they have a real chance to believe and
be saved.

What does our exegetical examination mean for the tension between proclaiming and discipling? If we bear in mind four main
points, the tension will be lessened if not resolved.

First, as an end God directs us to bring men to faith and obedience.
We are not sent out to conduct a token search for lost sheep, to beat
the bushes, and return empty-handed. We are sent to bring back to
the Father's house His beloved lost sons and daughters.

In evangelism we tell in gratitude what God has done for us, but
evangelism is not an exercise to demonstrate our gratitude. We are
sent out through God's grace to reconcile sinners to God.

Often it happens that, after we have done our best to find lost
sheep, we return empty-handed. The sheep did not want to be found.
They fled on our approach, or we looked for them in the wrong
ravines. Under these circumstances we had better say frankly that we
have failed, rather than to indulge in any circumlocution to the effect
that God does not want us to find sheep. He merely wants us to be
faithful proclaimers.

On the contrary, if there is anything to which the entire New
Testament witnesses, it is that God sends us to find the lost. That
is what our Lord was sent to do. That is what He in turn sends us to
do. That is what missions is all about. It is a vast continuous operation to find lost children and bring them back to their Father's
house.

If any are carrying on missions of proclamation as *complete* mission, they cannot justify it from the Bible. The purpose of

missions is bringing men to a saving knowledge of Jesus Christ, the
Lord.

Second, as a means to discipling the nations, God wants all men to
hear the gospel, but not just to hear. That is possibly a worse heresy
than denying the virgin birth. As a first step, as a means to an end, He
does want them to hear. The proclamation of the gospel is always a
means. It must never be elevated to an end. It is a means to bring all
nations to faith and obedience. As a means it is clearly commanded.

Third, each nation in the world is a mosaic of peoples, many of
them resistant, some of them responsive. Every family in the world
has its more and less responsive members. Some are hostile, some
friendly, to the Word of life. All must hear; but resources and time
should be concentrated on those who welcome the messenger. The
missionary nurse, in order to be faithful, should know which of her
many patients come from segments of society that are open to the
gospel and which from those that are closed. The apostles were to
enter every village and perhaps knock on every door, but they were to
tarry and teach only where interest was so high that they were fed and
housed. The minister in an American city rightly gives most of his
time to those who respond favorably to his church and his message.
Otherwise he would be starving the sheep which come to his fold
while pursuing those which flee at his approach.

This third theological principle will seldom, if ever, mean leaving a
whole country. It is much more likely to mean intelligent cultivation of
those segments of its population from which men and women have
accepted Jesus Christ as Savior from the guilt and power of sin.
Cultivation may on occasion mean evangelism and on occasion mean
service. It may, indeed, sometimes mean joining in a revolution. The
Reformation in Scotland was also a throwing off of the political and
military rule of Mary Queen of Scots. Reformation leaders did not
hesitate to support with money and swords that revolution. The
revolutionaries under Oliver Cromwell are another case in point.
Cultivation of a responsive segment means working among those who
are accepting Jesus Christ as Lord in the fellowship of His Church and
the vocations of the common life.

With these three meanings bright in our thinking, we are ready for
the fourth: Scripture leaves us free to use our common sense as to how
to manipulate the means to achieve the biblical end, but gives us no
freedom to turn the means into the end. Let us consider three
practical applications of this fourth main meaning.

1. *We missionaries must not become sentimentally attached to "our work" into which we have poured ten, twenty, or even thirty years of our lives.* We must regard our residences as foxholes. We must not air-condition them. Our establishments, built up during the periods of seed sowing and germination, are as expendable as tanks on a battlefield. We must not tearfully insist that we are forever tied to unfruitful populations. Shaking off the dust against rebellious populations must always remain a sobering biblical possibility to be exercised with tears, under the direction of the Holy Spirit, and with due caution, but *exercised.* Proclamation in advance of church establishment should be regarded as a probe. We probe to see if, after allowing time for germination and maturation, there is harvest in this place. If not, we know the Lord's command.

2. *Mission executives and missionaries, remembering the end and the means as they look at various populations, must constantly weigh probabilities of their obedience in the light of their resources and constantly seek the Spirit's leading as to where to go.* Ministers working in America see resistant and responsive sections of their parishes. They do not rejoice in by-passing hard, rebellious homes or parts of town or neglected Spanish, black, or pagan white populations where juvenile delinquency flourishes. Yet they, like Paul, often do turn from those who reject the Word of life and give their limited time to those who hear and come to their churches. In America, ministers constantly weigh probabilities of reception in the light of limited resources.

3. *Executives, theologians, and ministers in America can make sure that they are carrying on biblically sound mission abroad.* Let me speak directly to them. You, my friends, stand apart from the problem. You are not emotionally involved. You have not poured your life into some static situation. Yet the mission is yours. You are not just sending money to help some brave missionary do *his* work. You and he together are working in obedience to God. You and he both are carrying out mission on a biblical basis, keeping clear that the *end* is bringing the multitudinous *ethnē* to faith and obedience, while the *means* is preaching the gospel to all. You and the missionary together can consider questions like these:

How much church growth have we gotten? Have we sowed the seed here long enough?

Are we using the right methods to persuade men to accept Christ?

Are others communicating the gospel better than we? If so, why?

Are there more responsive sections in this population? If so, where?

Answering these questions for each mission field in which a society labors will require much research. Three to 5 percent of the total resources of most missionary societies should be spent in systematic research about church growth. Only then will the fields and the home bases be able to make realistic assessments and act accordingly.

As I close I must hold up the Revelation of Saint John: "The Revelation of Jesus Christ, which God gave Him to show to His bond-servants" (1:1). In this He solemnly affirms:

> I am the Alpha and the Omega, the beginning and the end . . . the cowardly and unbelieving and abominable and murderers and immoral persons and sorcerers and idolaters and all liars, their part will be in the lake that burns with fire and brimstone, which is the second death. [Rev. 21:6, 8]

Make whatever allowance you will for these words being figures of speech or symbolic; nevertheless, such is the state of the unsaved of every land and of the three billion who today owe Him no allegiance and probably do not even know His name. Do not their urgent needs drive us to proclaim everywhere the message through which alone deliverance can be found, remembering ever that the goal is so to proclaim that they do obey, and to proclaim where they do become Christians? Oh, that the Spirit might be so poured out from on high that many ministers would be constrained to leave their surfeited congregations; that overseas many missionaries, leaving churches and schools to the care of resident nationals, might multiply new churches in some unreached and receptive *ethnos*. Thus, the Church in six continents would by personal obedience emphasize the reality of the gospel, preach it everywhere, and disciple the families of mankind until not one section of a city or one village in a countryside remained without its church.

It is not sufficient to be doing a work good in itself while the Master's Great Commission is unfulfilled. What Christ commanded nineteen hundred years ago and what is now possible is to disciple *ta ethnē*, the peoples, the tribes. The urgent need of the world underlines the obvious duty of the Household of God to proclaim Christ, baptize believers, and multiply churches. To those ends Christians should devote themselves, praying to God for the strength needed and being confident that if they do so, He will greet them on that day with, "Well done, good and faithful slave; . . . enter into the joy of your master" (Matt. 25:21).

The momentous decisions required to implement these theological convictions will not be easy, but they will be blessed by God.

7

Ambiguity, Theology, and Church Growth

In the midst of today's whirlpool of theological opinion, ambiguity often causes the gospel to limp where it should run. When a few bishops of the Episcopal Church are publicly charged with heresy, when Protestants are drawn into opposing camps, and when Roman Catholics find themselves bewildered in a plethora of conflicting pronouncements, then ambiguity is obviously present. Clarity of vision is greatly needed. Momentous decisions will be required to achieve it.

In the very day churches can multiply, they stand still, confused about their task. Words about mission are used in new senses; it is fashionable, and perhaps profitable, to be obscure. In some quarters, obscurity is mistaken for profundity. Take Paul Tillich's vague dictum that all mankind which is not yet Christian is "the latent Church," and its cognate doctrine that all men have been reconciled to God by the death of Christ, but do not yet know it. Many Christians and some missiologists quote this with approval. But what do they mean by these ambiguous phrases?

If they intend simply to diminish the distance between Christian and non-Christian in the hope of more conversation, or to assert that Christ died for all men, or to recall that God so loved the world that He gave His only Son, this is one thing. But if they mean that there is salvation in the latent Church, this is something else. In an exact sense, have men been reconciled to God until each has accepted the proffered reconciliation for himself?

If the phrase *latent Church* means no more than "let us recognize each man as a potential Christian," as Douglas Webster says in *Unchanging Mission*, most Christians will agree; but unfortunately much more than this is usually meant. If non-Christians are in the latent Church, then they are already in some kind of a Church. To quote Hans-Werner Gensichen,

> If the eternal Logos is "the true light that enlightens every man" (John 1:9), the mission can have no other aim than to identify and reinforce the vestiges of Christ in the religions and thus lead the people in those religions to a better understanding of their own religious existence. Raymondo Pannikar has described the ultimate goal of this process in terms of Christ being born again in the womb of each non-Christian religion.[1]

With such meanings of "the latent Church" most Christians will heartily disagree.

It is particularly important that those advocating an irenic approach to other faiths clarify their position vis-à-vis the necessity for each man—if he desires salvation—to believe in Jesus Christ, openly confess His name, and unashamedly live as a responsible member of His Church. An irenic approach is one thing; religious relativism is entirely different.

We are not speaking about cultural adaptations. As the Church flows into *ethnos* after *ethnos*, it of necessity flows into different cultures. The Word of God comes to each *ethnos* in its own language, not Hebrew, Greek, or English. The Church is thus born from the womb of a new culture.

In one culture all Christians eat food with their fingers rather than with knives and forks. In another culture men and women live as members of tight communities, not as individuals. In cultural matters the Church can and must adapt. But concerning the worship of evil spirits, idolatry, atheism, agnosticism, or non-Christian scriptures which advocate these, Christianity can make no adaptation at all.

The communicator in most circumstances will be irenic, as was

1. Hans-Werner Gensichen, *Living Mission: The Test of Faith* (Philadelphia: Fortress, 1966), p. 61.

Paul on Mars' Hill; but he will always proclaim Christ crucified as the sole means of salvation.

A 1966 pronouncement of an important interdenominational organization says, "The role of leaven, of salt, of a redemptive remnant, of a servant who suffers, has come to be seen as more authentic and realistic than that of a triumphant sociological Christianity."[2] This sentence might mean that meeting human need (hunger, cold, ignorance, disease) is more truly Christian than adding men to the Lord and multiplying His churches. On the contrary, it might mean that the true Christian, when he distributes famine relief, baptizes men, or multiplies churches, must be humble, not arrogant. Which does it mean?

Are such terms (leaven, redemptive remnant, salt, and suffering servant) irenic middle-of-the-road phrases deliberately fashioned to hold together both ends of a distribution of Christians? Or are they radical new interpretations of Scripture deceptively draped in traditional language?

The issues are too grave for statements which intend one thing while seeming to say something quite different. Ambiguous statements divide Churches rather than unite them. This is particularly the case when many Christians, rightly or wrongly, suspect that the reins of power have been seized by those who have abandoned the faith—or reinterpreted it so radically that it is as good as abandoned. Ambiguous statements have in days past been used to blindfold the brethren until some years have rolled by.

In regard to all ambiguous theological statements about mission, we need to strip off the draperies and see what lies underneath. We have nothing to fear from new theological statements—if they are of God; but confused thinking is always open to the charge that it is deliberately foisted on the churches for ulterior motives. Drapery readily becomes camouflage.

Clarity of thinking in regard to the momentous decisions in mission is a crying need of our day. If churches are to remain God's churches, they must resolutely shun deception of all sorts. The less ambiguity and the more clarity in all our pronouncements, the better.

Some persons feel that Christianity as we have known it for two thousand years is coming to an end and realistic mission should therefore seek not propagation of existing irrelevant churches but

---

2. *Occasional Bulletin*, Missionary Research Library, vol. 17, no. 9 (September 1966): 9.

rather bringing all aspects of the world under a vaguely defined God's will, inside or outside the body of Christ. They should spell out their views of mission and seek support from those who agree. It would be hypocritical and deceitful of them to camouflage their views in emotion-laden, traditional language and seek support from Christians who believe mission is spreading the faith until those who are in Christ according to the Scriptures are present in considerable numbers in every ethnic unit—every people—of mankind. Clarity in theologies and policies of mission is an overriding need today.

Both parties concerned should make momentous decisions to clarify their pronouncements. Renouncing ambiguity and rephrasing convictions clearly is a hard task but it can be done. Since both sides concerned believe they are cleaving to the truth, their decisions will require not merely stating their position clearly but also gathering supporters who similarly believe and excluding support from those who do not agree. All this calls for costly decisions.

8

Ecumenical Decisions

As the Church of Jesus Christ spreads around the globe, it must necessarily exist in thousands of Particular Churches, locally separate from one another. Particular Churches may be whole denominations or clusters of congregations within a denomination, arising in one segment of society. In Zaire, for example, Baptist churches speaking a Mono language would be one Particular Church and those speaking Kikongo quite another Particular Church. These speak different languages and are composed of saints with very different cultural outlook, political allegiances, and levels of income and education. There are at least four Particular Lutheran Churches in India—one of Mala-Madiga origin, one of Uraon-Munda origin, one of Pariah-Sambava origin, and one of Santal origin.

Oneness in Christ

There ought to be no denial of oneness in Christ and no hostility or anger toward the other Particular Churches. Momentous decisions are obviously called for if this loving attitude is to become widespread.

The Particular Churches, realizing they are part of the Universal Church, the Body of Christ, the Household of God, ought to live in peace and unity, and gladly be about their Father's business. The Bible suggests clearly how the Particular Churches can live in harmony with other Particular Churches from which they necessarily differ. Romans 15:7 reads, "Receive ye one another, as Christ also received us to the glory of God" (KJV).

Paul was, of course, writing about individuals. He was counseling the church in Rome to receive men and women from other congregations as full Christian brothers and sisters. That some came from Jewish backgrounds and some from Gentile should make no difference. That some ate pork and some did not ought not to be considered an obstacle. Christ had received them all, so they should receive each other. Yes, Paul was writing about individuals from different backgrounds, different ethnic and linguistic units. But surely the principle that he is here emphasizing ought also to be used in regard to Particular Churches. These Particular Churches are very numerous. David B. Barrett says that in the six continents are found 20,800 denominations.[1] If to this number we add the Particular Churches that exist within so many large denominations from the Roman Catholic[2] to the Assemblies of God, it is clear that we are talking about fifty thousand or more Particular Churches.

These segments of the Church have all been received by Christ. All have statements of faith according to which they admit members and order their lives. Each statement of faith—without fail—gives Christ a preeminent place and accepts Him as God and Savior. Each of these thousands of segments of the Church is beyond doubt Christian. Consequently, Paul's counsel in the passage we are considering may properly be applied to Particular Churches. Christ has received them; hence, they ought to receive each other.

The Particular Churches can never unite on cultural forms, scriptural emphases which fit particular circumstances, and specific organizational molds which degrees of worldly prosperity or intellectual development make possible or necessary. They ought not to try to achieve uniformity in the adiaphora of churchly life, the outer trimmings and the changing forms. How, then, can they receive each other as validly Christian—as Christ's redeemed?

Romans 15:7 is the key. Christians, in all their diverse settings, all

---

1. David B. Barrett, ed., *World Christian Encyclopedia* (Nairobi: Oxford University Press, 1982), p. v.

2. "Individual young Churches, adorned with their own traditions, will have their own place in the ecclesiastical communion." Walter M. Abbott, S. J., ed., *The Documents of Vatican II* (New York: Association, 1966), p. 613. See also page 51 for Particular Churches.

their varied denominations, all their different emphases, are to receive each other exactly as Christ received them. This is how we (who have been received by Christ) can be different from each other, disagree with one another, and still be united in Him. Christ has accepted us with all our errors and imperfections. We must do the same with members of all other Particular Churches.

It is obvious that all whom Christ receives are in error on some things, or, more accurately, on many things. The Bible tells us that while we were yet sinners and were helpless, Christ died for us. All the Epistles bear eloquent witness that many among those early Christians were "babes in Christ." Around the world Christians sing in a thousand languages, "Just as I am, poor, wretched, blind."

God Incarnate received us while we were poor, so as to make us rich; and while we were blind, so as to give us sight; ought we not to receive our brothers and sisters who are similarly handicapped? The apostle Paul penned Romans 15:7 to tell us that the saints must do just that. That is the key to Christian unity. That is true ecumenicity—not to receive merely those who belong to our organization, our association, our council, but to receive all of any background who belong to Christ. Fifty thousand true Particular Churches do not break the unity of the Church.

We do not have to believe that others' error is the truth; we do have to receive them, while they are (we think) yet in error. They are fellow Christians, members of the Body, taking orders from the same Head. If they confess Christ according to the Scriptures and count the Bible as their rule of faith and practice, they are valid Christians. We are to receive them while they are, according to our understanding of the truth, still in error on some things.

How we rejoice that the Savior received us while we were "yet sinners"—still in error! If we had to be right about everything before the Lord would receive us, then indeed we would be forever lost. It is His righteousness which covers our sin and His forgiveness which makes us whole. His truth blots out our error and foretells the day when we shall know even as He now fully knows us.

Structural unity is not what this passage of the Bible teaches. Mention of a monolithic ecclesiological temple is entirely absent from this significant passage. Particular Churches have multiplied throughout the earth and will multiply still more as the myriad classes, tribes, and cultures of men turn to faith in Christ. Unless some one Church becomes a state church and the state enforces one uniform ecclesiological government on all the rest (an unlikely eventuality), the brotherhood of free Churches will include more and more Particular Churches.

This must not lead to bickerings, strife, party spirit, and churchly warfare. Against that outcome, Scripture says, "Receive one another, therefore, even as Christ has received you to the glory of God."

This must not mean carelessness in regard to the truth or a cynical conclusion that there is no ultimate truth, that all opinions are equally true and hence equally false. This must not mean an inclusiveness so great that whether one believes in Jesus Christ according to the Scriptures or in Marx, Krishna, or Mohammed makes no difference. We are speaking of members of Christ's Body who confess His name, accept the Bible as His infallible Word, and intend to measure the rightness of their beliefs by the revelation of His holy will. It was to that company, every member of which had been received by Christ, that Paul wrote. Therefore, Christians holding strong convictions and loving one another ought to make the momentous ecumenical decisions such convictions require. Neither end of the tension should alone be grasped. Those making momentous decisions must cleave to the truth while at the same time receiving one another. These are truly ecumenical decisions. They are momentous. They allow the multiplication of Particular Churches while maintaining unity in Christ. They believe in One Body *and* many members as different as the finger and the eye, the hair and the tongue.

Oneness in Relation to World Evangelism

What does all this have to do with world evangelization and discipling all the peoples of the globe? A great deal. Since Christ has received all members of all Particular Churches, all are parts of His Church which He has sent into the world to proclaim Him as Lord and Savior and to encourage men and women of all ethnic units to become His disciples and responsible members of His Church. All Christians march under that flag. That command (Rom. 16:25–26) rings in all their ears. All Christians are therefore allies in the evangelization of the world.

World evangelization necessarily speaks to two great classes of men—nominal Christians and non-Christians. Both need to make a personal decision to follow Christ.

Nominal Christians exist in all Particular Churches. In some they

may be a tenth of the total and in others nine-tenths. Many Particular
Churches evangelize their own nominals, teaching them the Scripture
and urging that they follow it meticulously. Many Particular
Churches, however, do not evangelize their nominals. After baptizing
them in infancy they allow them to grow up almost totally ignorant of
the Bible.

Recognizing this fact enables us to see that world evangelization is
not properly concerned with that evangelizing of one's own nominals,
which many Particular Churches do. It *is* properly concerned with the
evangelization of nominal Christians in those Particular Churches
which allow them to grow up thoroughly worldly men and women.
World evangelization must speak to the hundreds of millions of these
uncared-for nominals.

Whole missionary societies are organized to win converts from and
multiply churches among Particular Churches which are "wrong" on
certain points. Thus the Roman Catholic Paulist order was organized
to multiply Roman Catholic churches among Protestants. And many
Protestant missionary societies are hard at work in Latin America, the
Philippines, and other Roman Catholic nations, proclaiming the
gospel and adding to their congregation such as believe.

A hundred years ago all such action was regarded as unfriendly
and—by the churches losing members—as immoral. But today a
completely new mind-set is common. All such discipling is accepted
as, on the whole, a good development. Hundreds of missionary
societies are hard at work propagating the truest gospel they know.
This cannot be called evil. In regard to those being won it must be
observed that by and large only the nominals from various branches
of the church shift into other Particular Churches. Well-fed sheep
cannot be persuaded to go with a strange shepherd. But starving
sheep readily turn to anyone who gives them abundant food.

True ecumenicity welcomes this contemporary mind-set. True
ecumenicity is confident that passage from one Particular Church of
Christ to another Particular Church of Christ cannot be considered a
sin. Indeed it has much to commend it. If the person making the
transfer comes to a deeper knowledge of Christ, a more intelligent
obedience to His commands, and a greater understanding of His will,
then moving to the new Particular Church, far from being a sin, must
be termed a righteous act.

All this means that true ecumenicity rejoices in every Particular
Church proclaiming the truth as it sees it, and persuading all hearers

to accept that truth and become members of Christ's Body in that Particular Church.

But we shall not substitute such persuasion of nominal Christians for the evangelization of non-Christians, those belonging to non Christian religions—Secularism, Marxism, Islam, Hinduism, animism, Judaism, and Buddhism. The three billion non-Christians, rapidly becoming four billion, must remain the primary object of evangelization. These lost men and women must be found. These sons and daughters of God who are wasting their substance in riotous living in a far country must come back to their Father's house.

The three billion exist in a tremendous number of distinct segments. There are thousands of separate castes in India and other thousands of separate segments of society in China. Islam is famed for its multitudinous denominations, some of which, like the Shias and Sunnis in Lebanon, are often at war with each other. Each of these multitudinous segments of mankind must be effectively evangelized. This difficult task has been commanded by the eternal God (Rom. 16:25–26) who will give His servants power to make the momentous decisions required and carry them out.

In summary, true ecumenicity is essentially concerned with the spread of the gospel. The ecumenical Christian receives other Christians as Christ has already done, and then he and they in their own Particular Churches surge out to obey the Great Commission. They are commanded to disciple all the peoples of the earth (mathēteusate panta ta ethnē), and they will do whatever needs to be done to carry out that command. In places this will mean winning nominal Christians to ardent faith. In places it will mean winning agnostics and Secularists. In places it will mean bringing those who worship evil spirits and have no religious book at all to worship the Triune God and accept the revelation He has given us. And in yet other places it will mean long-continued evangelization of our non-Christian neighbors. True ecumenicity is ardently evangelistic.

9

Is the Great Commission God's Command?
Everett F. Harrison

As chapter 2 has set forth, momentous decisions in mission, based on the belief that world evangelization is God's command, must be made. Romans 16:25–26, Matthew 28:19, and similar passages are the authority for this belief. Until literary and historical criticism of the Bible spread through the Church, no one doubted this. The Roman Catholic missionary movement of the sixteenth and seventeenth centuries and the Protestant missionary movement of the nineteenth century were confident that they were carrying out a divine command.

However, as higher criticism became common and biblical scholarship began to be considered chiefly that which dealt with how biblical books assumed their canonical form, doubts multiplied as to whether God had really commanded world evangelization.

Everett F. Harrison, a noted New Testament scholar, dispels these doubts in this chapter. He proves that intelligent reading of the pertinent passages, and of allied Scripture whose authenticity has never been questioned, necessitates understanding them as voicing God's and Christ's command. All careful readers of the Bible will find this chapter (first published in Christianity Today) illuminating. It speaks to all those inclined to question the authenticity of the *passages concerned, and in particular to doubt that the risen Lord spoke the words recorded in Matthew 28:18–19 and that the early Church regarded the Great Commission as a motive for mission.*

Donald A. McGavran

How unfortunate it is that just when large sections of the world are increasingly receptive to the gospel message the Church is hampered by uncertainty in some quarters over divine authorization for its mission! We are told that it is unethical to subject people of other faiths to Christian propaganda, that the presence of missions is legitimate but their *proclamation* is not. In other words, to provide an example of Christian life is fine, but to attempt to convert is wrong.

This timid approach gets support from the assertion that the Great Commission did not originate with the risen Lord but was attributed to him by the young Church. After all, the Lord did not write the Gospels. They emerged a generation or so later. We are told that they should be understood primarily to reflect the ideas and practices of the Church, even though they doubtless contain some information about what Jesus said and did.

Transferring the Great Commission from the risen Lord to the Church weakens the commission, even if one acknowledges that the Church was not guilty of wrong-doing in attributing it to him. If the Lord did not voice the Great Commission, the way is open to question the legitimacy of aggressive evangelism. But if the commission does indeed go back to Christ, then on the basis of his universal authority he not only advocated but commanded a ministry of verbal witness to those who already had a faith of some kind. The Jews were committed to monotheism, as were the Samaritans, and the pagan world had gods aplenty.

The storm center of the debate is Matthew 28:18–20. Here the going forth to win all nations is said to have three elements: making disciples, baptizing them, and instructing them in the commandments of the Lord Jesus. The first item covers conversion, the second baptism (which implies conversion and denotes incorporation into the life and fellowship of the triune God), and the third the regulating and maturing of Christian life.

The Command to Evangelize

Our first task is to try to determine whether the Lord actually spoke the words about discipling the nations. By his own admission he was sent only to the lost sheep of the house of Israel (Matt. 15:24). In keeping with this limitation, when he sent out his disciples to preach and to heal during his own ministry he warned them against going to the Gentiles and to the Samaritans, charging them to restrict their work to Israel (Matt. 10:5, 6). At first glance, then, it may seem strange that in his final instructions he should set aside this restriction and command a ministry to all the nations.

But close examination reveals that it is not strange at all. Are we really prepared to believe that the Lord who showed such concern for Israel that he sent out his disciples to minister to the needs of the people (Matt. 10) felt so little concern for the world beyond that even after he had accomplished redemption for all mankind he failed to send the same men forth on a larger mission by an express command?

Even when he was concentrating on his own people, Jesus had repeatedly shown an interest in non-Israelites—healing the centurion's servant (Matt. 8:5–13), responding to the plea of the Canaanite woman for help (Matt. 15:21–28), predicting the dissemination of the Gospel to all nations throughout the world (Matt. 24:14; 26:13). But until his own nation had officially rejected him and until the basis for a worldwide proclamation of the Gospel had been laid in his death for all men and in his resurrection, concern for other nations had to be held in check. The enlargement of the scope of the disciples' operations after the resurrection is strictly in keeping with the mind of Christ.

Though Jesus had been reared in Galilee and during his ministry had spent most of his time there, he had avoided its Hellenistic areas. But now that his mission was completed and full redemption was accomplished, what was more fitting than his selection of Galilee as the locale for prescribing a worldwide mission?

It would be sheer desperation for the critic to maintain that the compassionate overtures our Lord made to non-Israelites during his ministry and his predictions of a worldwide mission were deliberately inserted into the record to prepare the way for Matthew 28:18–20. Suppose we take Matthew 26:13 as a test case. Passover was just at hand when Jesus attended a supper at Bethany and was anointed with expensive ointment. He accepted this ministration as a preparation for his burial (v. 12), then went on to state, "Truly, I say to you, wherever this gospel is preached in the whole world, what she has done will be told in memory of her." If in the oral stage the report of this incident had concluded with Jesus' word about his burial, what writer would have imagined that with such a mood upon him the Saviour would talk about the worldwide proclamation of the Gospel? The sheer unexpectedness of it suggests that this saying could have originated only with our Lord himself.

The word *truly* points in this direction also. A study of the Gospels reveals that Jesus alone is reported to have used this expression. In this respect it parallels the Son of Man sayings. Schlier remarks that in this word, placed as it is before the solemn "I say to you" of Jesus, "we have the whole of Christology in a nutshell." The Lord's own person guarantees the truth of his utterances. It should be noted that the parallel verse in Mark, 14:9, also has the expression.

A difficulty remains, however, for those who accept Matthew 28:19a as the words of the risen Lord. Would the early Church have been so tardy and even reluctant in taking the Gospel to the nations if the Master had commanded the apostles to do this very thing? The account in Acts shows concern for outreach only after several years had passed. Indeed, one might say that the Jerusalem church did little to promote Gentile evangelism in any direct way. Is this a valid objection?

It may be granted that outreach came somewhat slowly. Yet the contribution of the mother church was considerable, both in providing workers (e.g., Barnabas, Silas, and those who began the work at Antioch) and in clearing the way for the reception of Gentiles into the church without circumcision (Acts 15; cf. 11:18). The winning of Gentiles was acknowledged with praise to God (Acts 21:20).

Indeed, accusing the Jerusalem church of tardiness may be inaccurate. In his parting words to the apostles, Jesus named the spheres that would engage their witness—Jerusalem, Judea, Samaria, and the regions beyond—but laid down no timetable. It was essential to establish a strong base in Jerusalem. Luke's account shows how important this base was even for Paul, the leading missionary to the Gentiles, who kept up regular contact with it.

If the Jerusalem church had spread itself thin by early missionary endeavor in the Gentile world before it had made a solid impact on Jews in their own territory, its success in the wider field would have been seriously hampered. The question would naturally come up, If this new faith embodies the truth of God, why hasn't it been more successful among those who were supposedly prepared for it by centuries of promise and anticipation? There is something natural, if not inevitable, in the gradual extension of the Church's outreach—to the Jews of Jerusalem and Judea, to the mixed population of Samaria, then to the non-Jews of the world beyond. Note too that the impulse for the advance from the second to the third stage came by the direction of the Spirit in ever enlarging circles—the Ethiopian eunuch (chapter 8), the household of Cornelius (chapter 10), and the initiation of a large-scale missionary thrust among the Gentiles (chapter 13).

Surely the early Church sought guidance from Scripture, if for no other reason than that the Lord had based his instruction on it during the post-resurrection appearances. In many passages the Old Testament taught that the ingathering of the Gentiles must await the rejuvenation of Israel. James's use of Amos 9:11, 12 at the Jerusalem Council is instructive. He seems to have identified the emergence and growth of the Hebrew-Christian church with the promised rebuilding of *the booth of David* and on this basis proceeded to encourage the outreach to *all the nations*, the next stage in the Amos prophecy. The Acts and the Pauline epistles alike certify that there was no prejudice against having Gentiles in the Church (after all, Judaism was active in proselytizing them through the synagogue). However, some Jewish Christians were insisting that the practice of Judaism should prevail for the Church, namely, that these converts must be circumcised before being welcomed into the fellowship. In effect, this was to make them Jews before they could become Christians.

God chose to enlighten Peter on this matter first (Acts 10), showing him that the old distinction between Jew and Gentile as clean and unclean was no longer valid. In Peter's words, "He made no distinction between us and them, but cleansed their hearts by faith" (Acts 15:9). This was far more meaningful than a ritual purification by the rite of circumcision. Heavily influenced by Peter's experience at Caesarea, the Jerusalem Council decided that no burden should be put on Gentiles who came into the Church: faith in Christ was sufficient. This decision opened the way for a greatly expanded ministry both to God-fearers and to pagans.

Matthew 28:18–20 is not alone in stating a Great Commission that takes in all the nations. Luke 24:47 does the same (cf. Acts 1:8). But another source, one that is easily overlooked, is the commission given to the Apostle Paul (Gal. 1:16; Rom. 1:5; 11:13; cf. Acts 9:15; 22:21; 26:17, 18). Critics who are skeptical about accepting as the words of Jesus many of the statements attributed to him in the Gospels and who are cautious about accepting some of the data are quite ready to admit the testimony of Paul contained in his acknowledged letters. His call to the service of Christ with its specific commission to work among Gentiles is stated in the clearest fashion in his epistles and is confirmed by the passages in Acts. Evidently the early Church did not interpolate this item. It was known and accepted that the Lord Jesus, no later than two or three years after his resurrection, had intervened to transform and redirect the life of the persecutor. Are we to conclude, then, that the Lord commissioned Paul to minister to the Gentiles but gave no such responsibility to the apostles whom he had personally chosen and trained to communicate his Gospel to the world? It is strange that anyone would think the Church stumbled along for many years, only gradually seeing in the Gentiles a proper mission field (recall that Judaism had been seeing them as such for a long time), and then, feeling it needed the Lord's approval for what was now an accomplished fact, put the Great Commission into his mouth!

The commission given to Paul, while it featured the Gentiles, did not exclude Israel. With this in mind, the emphasis in Matthew 28:19 is seen to be not on all *the nations* but on *all* the nations. Israel is not being overlooked or excluded.

One cannot fairly appeal to Mark 16:15, 16 as the words of Jesus, since the whole passage (16:9–20) has inferior textual attestation. However, this portion at least reflects the belief of the Church at an early period that Jesus had commanded a universal proclamation of the Gospel to be followed by the baptism of those who believed. More to our purpose is the observation that if we had the original ending of Mark it would very likely contain something corresponding to Matthew 28:18–20. This inference is based on the fact that most of the substance of Mark is reproduced in Matthew. What supports the inference is the twofold mention in Mark of the plan of Jesus to meet his disciples in Galilee after his resurrection (Mark 14:28; 15:7). Galilee, of course, is the setting for the Great Commission as reported in Matthew.

The Command to Baptize

This element of the Great Commission must be included in our investigation, for if this one can be successfully challenged, the entire passage can more readily be set aside as not emanating from Jesus himself.

One such attempt made in the area of textual criticism is an article by F. C. Conybeare entitled, "The Eusebian Form of the Text Matthew 28:19."[1] He pointed out that in quoting this passage Eusebius usually made use of a shorter form that did not mention baptism. In only three citations did he quote the verse in its full form as we have it in our Bibles. It had to be granted, of course, that this was an isolated phenomenon, for otherwise the entire textual tradition consisting of manuscripts, versions, and patristic quotations failed to support the abbreviated form. Nevertheless the discovery was somewhat disconcerting. However, in an article entitled "The Lord's Command to Baptize," C. H. Chase showed that when Eusebius omitted the command to baptize in quoting the verse he did so because this portion of it was not germane to his discussion.[2] He noted further that this habit is common among other writers both ancient and modern. Consequently one can fairly maintain that Eusebius is not actually a witness for an abbreviated form of Matthew 28:19 that omits the words about baptism.

However, a more serious reason has been advanced for questioning that our Lord spoke the command to baptize, at least in the form Matthew gives. It is said to be inconceivable that the practice of the early Church, as reflected in the Book of Acts, would fail to follow the Master's command. That is to say, if he actually commanded baptism in the name of the Trinity, the failure of the Acts to report any baptism after this manner is inexplicable.

A reply can be suggested on the following order. What we find in Acts is simply Luke's report that on several occasions people were baptized in the name of Jesus Christ (2:38; 10:48) or in the name of the Lord Jesus (8:16; 19:5). The variation in the terminology—Jesus Christ and the Lord Jesus—is enough to warn us that this is not to be understood as a precise formula. In fact, it was intended not as a formula at all but as an indication that when the candidate confessed that sacred name, Jesus Christ was central to the new relationship that

1. *Zeitschrift für die neutestamentliche Wissenschaft* 2 (1901): 275–88.
2. *Journal of Theological Studies* 6 (July 1905): 481–512.

was being certified in the baptismal rite. "The fulness of Christ's saving work is contained in his name."[3]

But what of the trinitarian terminology in Matthew 28:19? Is it intended, in contrast to the short form noted above, to serve as a liturgical guide, specifying the words to be used by those who administer baptism? Jesus did not say, "You are to baptize, saying, 'I baptize you in the name of the Father and of the Son and of the Holy Spirit.'" Therefore we can reasonably maintain that just as the shorter expression indicates that the convert is to recognize the crucial importance of Christ for salvation, the longer form is meant to show that those who administer the rite are to communicate to the candidates for baptism that they are being brought into relationship with the whole Godhead conceived as a unity (note that *name*, not *names*, occurs here).

However this may be, one has to grant that by the third or fourth generation thereafter, fairly early in the second century, the Lord's command in Matthew about baptism *was* treated as a liturgical formula, for directions are given for administering baptism by using these words (*Didache* chapter 7). In the second of two references it is stated that if running water is not available, the one who performs the rite is to pour water three times on the head "in the name of the Father, Son, and Holy Spirit." So it may well be that the practice of the Church prior to this time followed the same pattern. Of great interest is the fact that the *Didache* also speaks of those who have been baptized "in the Lord's name" (chapter 9). Since it is highly unlikely that two differing formulas would be recognized in the one document, the latter expression must indicate the significance of baptism, reflecting the terminology used in the Book of Acts. So there is no more need to see contradiction between Matthew 28:19 and the language of Acts than to see it between the two passages in the *Didache*.

We come to a more delicate question. Is it essential to hold that in Matthew 28:19 we have the very words of the risen Lord? Chase is willing to concede that the words in Matthew need not be identical with the actual words of Jesus. On principle, one is obliged to agree, for where we have parallel accounts in the Synoptic Gospels the language frequently differs. So, for example, Mark reports that at the

3. *Theological Dictionary of the New Testament*, vol. 5, p. 273.

Last Supper Jesus said to his own, "This is my blood of the covenant, which is poured out for many" (Mark 14:24), whereas Matthew has, "For this is my blood of the covenant, which is poured out for many for the forgiveness of sins" (Matt. 26:28). However, the language in Matthew 28:19 about baptism is such that one can hardly imagine anything different coming from the lips of Jesus. What else could he have said that would be similar but different?

If one is inclined to stumble over the trinitarian character of the expression, feeling that it is too early for such a statement to be made, especially since Jesus had not used such language prior to the cross, then it is wise to reflect on the fact that less than thirty years later the Apostle Paul penned a benediction that has a trinitarian framework (II Cor. 13:14). It is impossible to prove that he is indebted to the language of Jesus for this, but nevertheless it is likely that the triune terminology was familiar to those who received the letter, which in turn tends to carry back the source of the conception to the very beginning of the Church's life. After all, the triune God figured in the baptism of Jesus at the Jordan (Matt. 3:13–17), and the Saviour's teaching had included the Spirit along with the Father (John 14:16, 17; Luke 12:10–12).

The Command to Catechize

Rounding out the Great Commission is the injunction to teach those who have been evangelized and baptized. There was much for converts to learn—about the Lord himself, about the Scriptures that foretold his coming and his redemptive work, and about the obligations of discipleship. It is not surprising, then, that immediately after the 3,000 Pentecost converts were baptized they were placed under the instruction of the apostles (Acts. 2:42). Incidentally, this very obligation meant that the apostles were not free to fan out to remote regions of Palestine and beyond. The apostles could not be expected to impart in a few days what it had taken them the greater part of three years to acquire. And the Spirit was adding more to their store of knowledge (John 16:13).

To be sure, it is disappointing that we have no information at this point in Acts about the content of the teaching. Some scholars, especially those who take a rigid form-critical approach to the Gospels, have questioned the existence of any considerable body of teaching derived from the Lord himself and passed on through the apostles to the Church. Instead, they have persuaded themselves that the Church, faced with the need to instruct its members, took the few things that were remembered and greatly added to them, so that our Gospels represent the final stages of the growth of the tradition. The effort to arrive at the authentic words of Jesus in the Gospels and separate them from the contribution of the Church involves tremendous uncertainties. No wonder those who are engaged in it fail to agree among themselves even about the criteria to be used.

It would be cavalier to dismiss the difficulties that beset one who insists that the exact words of Jesus are reproduced in Matthew 28:18–20. The vocabulary is distinctly Matthean at several points. It is enough to maintain that we have a directive from the risen Lord himself rather than a late formulation by the Church. One is bound to be impressed that all the Gospels have a command of some sort attributed to the Saviour (assuming that the original ending of Mark as well as the so-called long ending had it also), and this testimony is supplemented by Acts 1:8. Since the Matthean passage relates to a scene at which 500 brethren may have been present (I Cor. 15:6), the certification of our Lord's commission must have been singularly impressive for all concerned and for those to whom the recollection of the scene was imparted.

We have ample reason to be convinced that behind the Great Commission stands the authority of the person of Jesus and his plain, insistent direction to his Church. Christ is cause, not effect; he is subject, not object. The Church is his own ("my church," Matthew 16:18), and he prescribed in advance how it was to be nourished and guided, even by the words of truth that he had spoken, words that the Holy Spirit had impressed on those who were now equipped to communicate them to others.

On reflection one can readily see that all three parts of the Great Commission are fundamental to the Church's life and work. The first leads on to the second and the second to the third. Together they form a perfect trilogy, a fitting counterpart to the Trinity itself.

Everett F. Harrison is professor emeritus of New Testament, Fuller Seminary, Pasadena, California, having taught there since 1947. He has theological degrees from Princeton and Dallas seminaries and the Ph.D. from the University of Pennsylvania. He is the author of five books and edited "Baker's Dictionary of Theology."

Part 2

Momentous Decisions about the Human Mosaic

10

The Hottest Race Issue in the World

In the global village in which we all live many if not most countries face varying forms of racism. Some pieces of the mosaic of mankind are grievously oppressed by the others. The strong pieces act unjustly toward the weak pieces. American Christians concerned to spread brotherhood, justice, and peace are acutely conscious of the racial issues in these United States. They are, alas, too frequently unaware of the much larger racial issues in some other countries. We hear a great deal about the small instances of racism in the southern tip of Africa but nothing of the enormous racism and terrible injustice which affects 150 million of God's children in the subcontinent of India. To those entrenched evils we now turn. They will require numerous decisions in mission.

Racism and the Indian Caste System

Exact understanding of the Indian caste system requires that we see its two distinct parts—its theological foundations and its local manifestations. Each requires different treatment by Christians. These same parts are also to be distinguished in every country of the world where racism of any sort manifests itself. All racism has the same two parts.

Among men of all ages and races the strong have controlled the weak and have rewarded themselves much more richly. Key players in professional football teams are paid millions. Ordinary players receive thousands. Heads of corporations live like lords, their employees like ordinary people. In 1066, when in the Battle of Hastings the Normans conquered the Saxons, they became the rulers of England. They reduced the Saxons to serfdom. They called them Saxon swine and treated them as such. They portrayed them as stupid, ugly, and vicious. With the passage of a couple hundred years, however, the distinctions between the Normans and the Saxons largely evaporated, and the time came when England proudly referred to itself as an Anglo-Saxon nation. The strong seldom are able to pass on their power and privileges to later generations. Thus local manifestations of racism, grievous and hurtful though they be, have tended to be short-lived. In North America from the descendants of the slaves of 1862 and from the sinfully oppressed blacks of a century later we shall doubtless elect a president or vice president of the United States some day.

However, occasionally the strong, the conquerors, developed and organized a religion which declared that God created them as superiors and created the conquered as permanent inferiors. Thus the local manifestations of racism were transformed into rock-hard theological or ideological foundations which were and are the antithesis of Christian brotherhood.

Precisely this happened in India some four thousand years ago. The white Aryans pouring down into India through Afghanistan conquered the dark-skinned Dravidians who then populated India. The Aryans reduced the Dravidians to serfdom and called them *dasyus* or slaves. Then one of the authors of the Rig Veda composed a hymn in which he stated that God had created the Aryan priests from His head, the Aryan warriors from His arms, the Aryan merchants and landowners from His thighs, and the Dravidian serfs from His feet. In short, God had created four orders of humanity. The white Aryans were the superior castes, and the Dravidians were the inferiors.

Each of the four castes which the writer described proliferated into hundreds of separate castes. Thus today there are hundreds of distinct priestly castes (Brahmans), hundreds of distinct warrior castes (Kshatriyas), hundreds of merchant and landowning castes, and hundreds of Sudra or inferior castes. In addition there are hundreds of distinct scheduled castes. These used to be called untouchables and were regarded as outside the pale of Hinduism. They were denied entry into Hindu temples. In south India their very shadow conveyed impurity. In the Himalaya Mountains they were ordered never to wear clothing below the mid-thigh, and in the south tip of India their men and women were ordered never to wear clothing above the waist. All these local manifestations of unjust treatment rested on the rock-hard theological foundations that God had created them as inferiors, as different from the respectable castes as cats are from lions.

A thousand years later the author of the Bhagavad Gita, after describing the four castes and the duties of each, wrote that the members of each caste should perform *their own duty*, even if they could perform the duty of another caste better. It was clear that members of the inferior castes should always humbly serve the superior castes, even if by virtue of mind or body they could teach or command armies.

About the same time the doctrines of karma and rebirth were perfected. According to the doctrine of Karma, each person constantly acts. If his action is good, he earns merit; if his action is bad, he earns demerit. Furthermore, the doctrine of rebirth declares that every soul is constantly reborn in a new body. If the balance of his eternal account is plus, he is born up the social scale. If it is minus, he is born down the social scale. Thus a man of the Sudra or inferior caste, if he humbly serves the upper castes, accumulates merit. If he seeks to improve his status or begins to act like a member of the upper castes, he is reborn further down the social scale. According to the Ramayana, a Sudra who dared to listen to sacred scripture intended only for the superior castes was to have molten lead poured into his ears. He would never hear anything again.

In Germany and to some extent in other parts of Europe in the last decades of the nineteenth century a "scientific" doctrine arose which declared that the dark-skinned races were less able, less intelligent, less vigorous races and that the white race was clearly the superior race among all men. This was proved by the ease with which it had dominated the rest of the world. The Nazis held that the Germans were the most superior of the white races. Here the foundation was not religious. It was rather ideological. This theory was, nevertheless, widely believed.

The battle for brotherhood must constantly recognize these two forms of racism. The principal enemy of brotherhood is the theological foundation of racism. Local manifestations of the strong controlling and oppressing the weak, although regrettable, must be recognized as of much less importance. But if brotherhood is to obtain around the world, the ideological and theological foundations of racism must be destroyed. If justice is to prevail (a justice based on the belief that all men are created free and equal), then the biblical account of the creation of man must be believed—namely, that God created one man, Adam, in His own image and that from that one man all races are descended. Because men have one common ancestor, Adam, they are all brothers. Those who battle for justice and brotherhood will, of course, seek to soften or eradicate local manifestations of unjust behavior. But they must recognize that if the theological foundations of racism are not eradicated, any improvement in local manifestations will be at best a small and temporary advance.

In India more than six hundred million men and women hold firmly to the belief that God has created man in four great molds or races. While the government of India and many educated Indians are busy at work trying to diminish the handicaps and oppressions under which the Sudras and the former untouchables have suffered, the theological foundations are never attacked or renounced.

It is as if the white population in Mississippi were to say, "The black population here should, of course, be given enough to eat, at least some education, indoor plumbing, electric light, and some of the amenities of life. But they are less able, less responsible, less moral than we whites and will always remain so, no matter how many local manifestations of oppression are removed."

In India the cause of justice and brotherhood can be furthered by leading multitudes of the respectable castes to recognize that the head-shoulders-thighs-and-feet theory was simply an effective self-serving device of the conquering Aryans and must be renounced. No amount of concessions made to men and women of the inferior castes will do any permanent good as long as the theological foundations of the caste system remain intact. If one believes in a sanctified and legalized racism, it makes little difference if the inferiors are given free college education and guaranteed seats in the state and national legislatures.

The Caste System and the Church

For the past two hundred years Christians from America, England, and other western lands have gone to India as missionaries of the gospel. They were concerned to find and save the lost. They intended to multiply churches of the redeemed among the vast populations in India. Baptists, Methodists, Anglicans, Presbyterians, Lutherans, Mennonites, and many other denominations each sent out hundreds of lifetime missionaries and over the years poured hundreds of millions of dollars into the evangelization of that great subcontinent.

As Christianity thus flooded into every district and subdistrict in India, what effect did the caste system have on its acceptance and spread? The answer to this question is of great significance to those fighting for brotherhood.

Roman Catholic missionaries tended to encourage men and women of the multitudinous ethnic units (castes) to follow Christ while remaining ethnically very much themselves. In *Hindu Manners, Customs, and Ceremonies*, we read: "Roman Catholicism is able to prevail among the Hindus more rapidly and easily, by reason of its policy of tolerating among its converts the customs of caste and social observances."[1]

The same was true in Protestant missions before 1805. After that date, however, Protestant missions insisted that when men and women became Christians, they must renounce their caste and eat with and worship with converts from any caste. Hindus immediately devised a most effective way of preventing conversion. They ruled that whenever anyone became a Christian (renounced his caste), he was to be ruthlessly outcasted. From the moment of his baptism on, no one of his own people would eat with him, smoke with him, give him a drink, or allow him to come into his home. His spouse would immediately leave the house. His children would have to seek spouses from the Christian community. No one of his former community would dare to give him a daughter-in-law or son-in-law.

The result of this policy has been dramatic. Conversions from the respectable castes and most of the inferior castes have been exceedingly rare—as rare as the conversion of Muslims in Muslim countries. Very occasionally some man of a superior caste would become a

---

1. Jean Antoine DuBois, *Hindu Manners, Customs, and Ceremonies* (Oxford: Clarendon, 1899), p. xxvii.

Christian. But the process was so infrequent that congregations which depended upon one-by-one conversion grew very, very slowly.

However, here and there some member of one of the untouchable castes or of an aboriginal tribe, on becoming a Christian, continued to live with his caste fellows and within a short space of time was able to bring hundreds of families to join him. When this occurred, his caste fellows at once said, "Oh, we can become Christians while we remain ethnically ourselves." Ostracism is a fearful weapon when exercised against a single person. It is, however, much less fearsome when exercised against a group of several hundred families. If one of them needs food or water or fire, he can get it quite easily from his own people, now Christians, in the neighborhood. When he dies, his own people will dig the grave and bury him.

So here and there across India castewise movements to Christ have flourished—but always among the lowest castes. Hundreds of thousands from some twenty-one castes have become Christians. In the Punjab hundreds of thousands of Churahs moved to Christian faith. In southern India Nadars, Pariahs, Malas, Madigas, and some other castes became Christians by the tens of thousands. Thus in India as a whole the church is composed largely of converts from the bottommost castes.

This fact would not be seen by a casual visitor from the west. He would meet with the educated Christian leaders who all speak good English. They and their fathers have been educated in mission schools and colleges. Many of them now hold government positions and are teachers in schools and colleges or businessmen of one sort and another. They and American Christians rejoice in their social progress, which demonstrates so clearly that the inherent abilities of men and women from the depressed classes are just as good as the inherent abilities of members of the respectable castes.

Nevertheless, six hundred million members of the respectable castes *perceive* Christians as a very low-caste community. They remember that the parents, grandparents, or great-grandparents of the million or so educated Christians were, after all, members of the lowest castes of Hinduism before they became Christians. To "become Christian" is perceived by respectable-caste Hindus as becoming a member of an exceedingly low segment of society.

Consequently, although respectable-caste Hindus hear the gospel with great pleasure and often have the highest respect for the Lord

Jesus Christ, they very, very seldom "become Christians"—that is, "join existing churches."

If in Alabama all the whites and nine-tenths of the blacks were non-Christians, one-tenth of the blacks had become Christians, and Christ was proclaimed in such a way as to make following Christ mean joining a black church, very, very few whites would "become Christians."

Although this picture of the church in India is exact, two notable exceptions must be briefly mentioned. In the extreme southwest tip of India there are some four million members of the Syrian church. These are converts from the upper castes who were won centuries ago. The first of them were probably won by the apostle Thomas around A.D. 56. But these Christians never intermarry with Christians from the other parts of India, for they believe that to do so would demean them. The other exception is the conversion of Sinic tribes in the hills of the extreme northeast tip of India, where it joins Burma and China. There some four million of these tribals have become Christians. With the exception of these eight million, the remaining sixteen million Christians in India can be correctly understood as having come in at least 98 percent from the bottommost ranks of the caste system.

Modern India and Caste

In the west the myth has been assiduously spread that in modern India caste has ceased to exist. In colleges and universities high- and low-caste people eat together at a common table. In trains and buses people of all castes rub shoulders with each other as they travel. "Caste" has become a dirty word, and the government is giving millions of dollars a year in scholarships for high school and college to promising boys and girls of the scheduled castes (former untouchables).

Since the government is taking this enlightened view toward caste, some westerners exclaim, "Should not Christian leaders in India all the more insist that in the church all converts from all castes must mix freely together forming a new community—the redeemed of Christ?"

The myth referred to must be seen as a myth. Actually 150 million souls are still regarded as the bottommost ranks of decent society. The landless laborers are still landless. Villages where the scheduled castes live separated from the residences of respectable people are still made up chiefly of hovels. Young men and women who have received scholarships in colleges frequently find great difficulty in getting jobs. Members of the respectable castes still control most of life in India. Organizations of educated scheduled-caste leaders frequently declare that the depressed castes must renounce Hinduism and the caste system and convert to Christianity, Islam, Buddhism, or some other religion. Until the 150 million embrace a religion which has a firm theological foundation demanding brotherhood, they will remain forever inferior. The poverty and squalor of "untouchable" villages results from the belief that God has created these people as permanently, racially inferior. No amount of change in behavior toward members of the scheduled castes will change the rock-hard theological foundations of caste.

It is worth remembering that while the great Mohandas K. Gandhi fought a desperate battle to keep the untouchables (whom he called harijans) within the fold of Hinduism, he said in effect, "I believe in the caste system—in the four orders of humanity—but I insist that we must treat the scheduled castes better." In cities the scheduled castes have been treated somewhat better. In the anonymity of great cities it is difficult to recognize who are persons of the respectable castes and who are the former untouchables. They all look very much alike. But once the visitor gets five miles away from any city out into village India, where 80 percent of the population still lives, there he discovers that very little change has taken place in the physical, mental, and social conditions of the oppressed 150 million.

A magazine, *Dalit Voice*, is being published in India. The word *dalit* means fallen. The "voice of the fallen" constantly pleads the cause of the oppressed 150 million. Christians in America interested in the battle for brotherhood should subscribe to *Dalit Voice*, Dalit Sahitya Akademy, 109 7th Cross, Palace Lower Orchards, Bangalore 560 003, India. In this magazine they will read a factual, unvarnished description of the actual situation.

Battling Oppression in India

This situation raises two questions for American Christians and missionary societies. First, what should American Christians do in regard to the entrenched racism in India? Four answers can be given to this question. First, they must recognize that racism still exists in America and many other lands. Some of the greatest, wealthiest, and most cultured lands on earth exhibit racism. So while American

Christians will combat racism in India, they will at the same time respect and honor that great nation.

Second, they must recognize that eroding the theological foundations of caste is much more important than diminishing local practices. Both tasks must, of course, be carried out. Both will take many years, possibly—if Christ tarries—many centuries. However, merely working to diminish the worst local manifestations, while leaving the theological foundations intact, is a fatally flawed procedure. The greatest contribution which American Christians can make to the spread of brotherhood anywhere is to multiply congregations of men and women who believe the Bible to be the Word of God, who firmly believe that in Christ there is no Jew, no Greek, no slave, no free, no male, no female. In Christ we are equal brothers and sisters. As these convictions come to be held by millions of people, women will gradually become fully enfranchised, slaves will gradually be freed, and the local manifestations of brotherhood will come into line with brotherhood's eternal God-built foundation.

Third, American Christians will therefore multiply their efforts in India and all continents of earth to find the lost, to bring them back to the Father's house, and to feed them on the infallible, authoritative, entirely true Word of God. This is the clear duty of American Christians.

Fourth, American Christians will also highlight, publicize, protest, and work to rectify the grievous and terrible local manifestations of racism in our great sister nation. As we do this, we will also work doubly hard to eradicate all traces of racism in the United States. We shall consciously pay much more attention to the tremendous racism in India than we do to the rather small manifestations of racism in South Africa. The battle for brotherhood rages in all parts of the global village. In most parts there are organizations committed to fight this battle. Christians should help such organizations and should frequently join them. While doing this, however, they should remember that such organizations usually are working to rectify local manifestations of oppression. Very seldom indeed are these secular organizations working to spread the biblical faith. Consequently, American Christians should not make support of such organizations their principal concern.

We now turn to pose and answer the second question. What should American Christians do in collaborating with our brothers and sisters in India? What should we help the Church in India do as it also battles racism? Our answer is clear. We should help the Church in India multiply congregations of the redeemed in every one of the thousands of castes in India. We should help it to realize that its main purpose is to seek and save the lost. The basic task is to multiply enormously the number of those who believe the Bible and its clear statement that all men are brothers, descendants of one father, equally sinners, and (when they believe on Jesus Christ) equally saved.

The Church in India needs to read the following quotation from an insightful American Christian newspaper, *Mission Alert*. In a 1984 issue Dennis Scott says:

> Occasionally I am asked why I talk about "Black churches," "Spanish churches," "Cambodian churches," or "Appalachian churches."
>
> "Why can't all God's people worship together?"
>
> "Why don't you just start one church and invite everybody?"
>
> "What we need is an 'integrated' church, with God's people showing the world that they love each other, regardless of the color of their skin, or their cultural background."
>
> . . . I do long for that time when all God's people will join across all barriers and worship Him together in spirit and in truth. I believe that time is coming, and I greatly enjoy experiencing a little of it this side of heaven. I am convinced, however, that now God has another method of reaching the multitudes. . . . It is one thing for God's children to worship Him together, and another for His church to reach the lost. Church planting is not primarily for the saved, but for the lost. While the saved may enjoy worshipping God with fellow Christians from other cultural groups, it is becoming clear that people become Christians most readily when they do not have to cross cultural or ethnic barriers. People are most receptive to becoming Christian when they are approached by someone much like themselves. It is those who are lost that our strategy must be designed to reach. . . .
>
> The Great Commission does not give us the option of only reaching those who will "fit in" to our existing churches.

If in India "becoming a Christian" means joining another ethnic unit (and all existing churches are to caste Hindus another—and low-caste—ethnic unit), then very few members of the respectable castes are going to become Christians. If, however, becoming a

Christian means forming at first dozens and later hundreds of congregations of "our own kind of people," then the theological foundations of caste on which the entire structure depends will be eroded and replaced by Christian foundations.

Nothing will happen as long as the Church in India proclaims, "If you are going to become a Christian, you join us. We have risen above caste. In Christ there is no caste. We are in fact a new order of mankind." While we Christians say and believe this, Hindus perceive something quite different. They perceive the Christian community as a very low-caste community, no matter how educated its leaders become. That we Christians consider their perception erroneous is beside the point. They perceive the situation in that way and will continue to do so. Only the multiplication of congregations of Bible-believing Christians in hundreds of ethnic groups (castes) has any likelihood of eroding the theological foundations of caste.

The best way to win the battle for brotherhood in India is to win a hundred million or more of the ordinary citizens of that great land to ardent, biblical faith. One effective means of doing this is to broadcast the gospel beyond the present membership of existing churches. Broadcasters, using radio and motion pictures, reach hundreds of millions of respectable-caste Hindus. These frequently come to have very high regard for the Lord Jesus Christ and for the Bible as God's Word. If these broadcasters will now add to their programs an invitation for those who, through listening to radio, reading Christian literature, or seeing Christian motion pictures, have come to believe on the Lord Jesus Christ to form groups of their intimates, relatives, close friends, and neighbors, to meet together as Christ groups or home Bible-study groups, *then* millions of respectable-caste men and women will, I believe, become committed followers of the Savior.

This has already happened in China. After listening to broadcasts many millions of Chinese in every part of that great nation have become followers of Jesus Christ in house churches. Sometimes these are gatherings of five to ten families, sometimes of fifty or a hundred families. Some meet in secret. Others meet openly. Because getting Bibles has been almost impossible, members of such house churches copy out by hand various books of the Bible—the Gospels, Romans, Philippians, and on and on.

The existing churches planted in the nineteenth and early twentieth centuries in China have had very little part in this ingathering. Indeed, they have often actively opposed it, although today they are beginning to welcome it. This great expansion is a result of Christian broadcasting. I believe that what has happened in China can happen in India and other sections of the world. The Word of God is powerful, a two-edged sword. As believers gather to form house churches based on the Word, unreached peoples *(ethnē)* will be reached. Populations which would under no circumstances join existing churches will begin to form new churches.

I believe, therefore, that in India the men and women of the respectable castes will be invited to form home Bible studies, Christ groups, or house churches in their own neighborhoods where they can become followers of Christ without "joining another people."

As this happens, the longest step toward brotherhood will be taken. As they put away all other religious books and read only the Bible as God's Word they will come to believe that God has created the entire human race from one man, made in God's image. So all men and women, descendants of one father, are therefore brothers and sisters. The distinctions of education, wealth, poverty, color, and occupation will, of course, remain, but these will be seen to be minor. For all those who accept the Bible as God's Word, the theological foundations of racism will be washed away. The local manifestations of racism, however, will continue for some time. The battle against racism will have been won, but the mopping-up operation will take some time.

Another thing which we should help the church in India to do is to work to diminish the local manifestations of racism. It has succeeded amazingly in reducing these among its educated leaders. Among the congregations which have grown through one-by-one conversion, caste consciousness is notable by its absence. However, in congregations which have grown through movements within a caste or tribe—and by far the larger number are of this latter sort—caste consciousness still continues, in many cases quite strongly. All kinds of frictions arise.

In a denomination made up of equal parts of converts from the Malas and the Madigas, let us say, if the moderator chosen is from one community, the other community will constantly feel mistreated. A Nadar Christian leader tends to believe that Nadars make better pastors than Pariahs. In a diocese of the Church of South India in Kerala, where a bishop who is a Syrian by racial background has been elected, the Christians from the scheduled castes are (in 1984) up in arms. The churches in India need to remember that once the theological foundation of caste is gone, local manifestations of injustice and racism will yield to Christian pressure. It may take years, decades, or even longer; but God's will *will* prevail.

In conclusion we need to remember that the Great Commission is very clear on this point. It says in Hindi, "Sab jatiyon ko chela karo" (disciple all castes). As this is done, the battle for brotherhood will be won.

Since Christian leaders in India and North America are so adamantly opposed to unjust, unbrotherly behavior, any implementation of the central directives of this chapter will require numerous decisions. Christian leaders in Europe, America, and India will need to believe that the multiplication of churches in every caste is the *only* way to assure significant growth in brotherhood. That the multiplication of churches *within* a given caste does often result in a continuation of local manifestations of racism must be recognized as a passing evil. Once the theological foundation is gone, the local manifestations will gradually diminish. Most Christian effort, therefore, must be focused on carrying out the Great Commission—"sab jatiyon ko chela karo." Let us apply those momentous decisions that direct the work of congregations, denominations, seminaries, missionary organizations, and missionaries to eroding the theological foundations of racism as well as diminishing its local manifestations. All this will require costly decisions and long-continued labor.

11

Is Group Ingathering Truly Christian?

Since 1955 when group ingathering (people movements, Christianization within tribes or castes) burst on the world of mission, it has stirred up much controversy and opposition. People movements (ingatherings *ethnos* by *ethnos)* have appeared dubiously Christian to many leaders. Many static denominations and missions, secure in their cocoon of rationalizing slow growth, do not see that people movements to Christ are an effective and thoroughly Christian mode of evangelism. They do not see that churches and missions will have to make momentous decisions if they are to use these Christ-blessed means.

Men and women like to become Christians without crossing linguistic, racial, and class lines. This missiological principle, sometimes called the homogeneous-unit theory, has been vigorously attacked from both the left and the right. These people believe that this principle encourages racism, segregation, and apartheid policies. They argue that it attacks the essential Christian teaching that in Christ we are all one.

Objections to Group Ingathering

Let us now consider five common objections to the discipling of ethnic units.

100

First, any group decision to accept Christ is suspect. Men are not saved by going along with the crowd. It is charged that when the one-by-one mode of the church of the first three centuries was abandoned in favor of the ruler deciding what his subjects should believe, the church deteriorated. Constantine's methods should be avoided. We want no more mass accessions.

Second, separating discipling from perfecting means that converts are offered salvation for very thin belief. They may accept Jesus as Savior but have no intention of obeying Him as Lord. This is cheap grace. It allows Americans to become Christians while maintaining hateful racist attitudes and animists to become Christian while continuing to practice witchcraft and sorcery.

Third, people movements create one-tribe, one-caste, or one-race congregations and denominations. Instead, Christians should move into churches which know no racial or class distinctions. It is charged that people-movement congregations ensure that sinful racist ideas continue. If we are to eliminate racism, we must insist that as converts accept Christ, they accept the doctrine that in Christ there is no Jew nor Gentile.

Fourth, people movements encourage nominalism. When nominalism is seen among Christians whose ancestors came to Christ through people movements, some churchmen exclaim, "The people-movement way of admitting converts is the cause of this nominality."

Fifth, people movements are men's work and planning. We should depend more on the action of the Holy Spirit.

The popularity of these five objections stems from the fact that in the third world the educated leaders of denominations usually belong to conglomerate congregations. In Asia and Africa they often belong to English-speaking congregations or have studied in English-medium seminaries. In these, most members and students came from many different economic classes, tribes, or other segments of mankind. Furthermore, they grew up in Christian households and so came to Christ not from non-Christian religions but one by one out of Christian households. Such educated nationals have great difficulty understanding how indigenous peoples (plural) become Christian. Their own experience has been how, in individualized westernized societies, men and women, boys and girls, become Christian one by one. They know very little of how in close-knit webs of relationships, in castes, tribes, and other homogeneous units men and women become Christians in a chain of group actions. Educated leaders think a chain of group decisions cannot happen and usually that it ought not to happen. At no point does westernization more greatly damage world evangelization.

One must point out that these objections arise very largely from pastors and missionaries serving nongrowing congregations and denominations. In 1956 the American Baptist Foreign Missionary Society sent *The Bridges of God*[1] to forty of its missionaries in many lands. Each was asked for an evaluation. As these came in, it was apparent that those whose churches were not growing were critical of the book, pointing out its many "errors" and the "obvious inexperience of its author." Those who were successfully propagating the gospel were cordially appreciative, and those nurturing and furthering people movements were loud in praise. Some years later a kindly general secretary of the society sent me copies of the evaluations. They are one of my prized possessions. They prove that to those knowing only the painfully slow growth of the one-by-one mode, people movements seem sinfully fast and superficial. If people movements are a legitimate and biblical form of church growth (John 4:7–42; Acts 11:20–26; Acts 17:12; etc.), then perhaps practitioners of the one-by-one mode should recognize that their objections may be defensive thinking. It is truly remarkable how rapidly advocates of these objections abandon them when *their* churches start to multiply.

The remarkable spread of the Christian faith among the proselytes in the many Jewish synagogues of the Roman world was, in today's terms, a people movement to Christ. Paul won both a minority of the racial Jews and a majority of the Gentile proselytes. And, while the Book of Acts and the Epistles do not tell us specifically that the proselytes in Antioch of Pisidia were related to the proselytes in Lystra, Derbe, and Iconium, it seems reasonable to believe that many such relationships (sometimes of blood and sometimes of other connections) did exist. These proselytes, we may assume, hearing that "our people" in nearby towns and cities had followed the Lord, were mightily inclined to listen to the gospel eagerly.

1. Donald A. McGavran, *The Bridges of God* (New York: Friendship, 1955).

Justifications for Encouraging People Movements

Having pointed out that the Bible includes several accounts of people movements, let us now answer objections to people movements.

The first objection is that going along with the crowd saves no one. I thoroughly agree on both biblical and pragmatic grounds. The Bible is clear that belief in Jesus Christ is necessary for salvation. Passage after passage affirms this. The Church has always taught this. To enter the kingdom of God, personal allegiance to the King is necessary.

People movements do not rise in going along with the crowd. The question, Shall we become Christians? is extensively debated—sometimes for years—before any group reaches a decision. The idea that in people movements some king or chief gives the order and all obediently follow like sheep is naive. People movements which rest on firmly held convictions of many men grow. In short, group decisions must not be unthinking acceptance of the leader's judgment. The group (whether it be out of a tribe, class, caste, or other segment of society) is made up of believing individuals. Each one has formed his own personal decision to follow Christ and accept the Bible as his rule of faith and practice.

True, the decision of each one is made easier by the knowledge that many of his comrades are making the same decision. Once a group of ten families or fifty is formed, its members, speaking to their relatives and intimates, encourage the formation of many other groups of new believers. Thus new congregations begin to form throughout that segment of society. But the only members of each group are individuals who—to some extent at least—do believe.

The second objection is that offering cheap grace is a poor way to carry out the Great Commission. In replying to this, one must note first that people-movement theory has never proposed a discipling in which Jesus is to be accepted not as Lord but only as Savior. Indeed, to non-Christians, becoming Christian means precisely turning from the lordship of gods and evil spirits to the lordship of Jesus Christ.

Then, too, a clear distinction must be made between biblical requirements for baptism for those becoming Christian, and requirements which appear desirable to the missionary or evangelist. Biblical commands must be obeyed. Other gods must be renounced. Idols must be burned or put away. Other religious books must be laid aside, and there must be repentance of sin. Cheap grace must not be offered.

But the Bible is silent about specific ethical actions: intermarriage with other ethnic groups; learning to read the Bible; living in a simple style; refusing to serve in the army; stopping scarification; eschewing gold rings, jewelry, or fashionable dress; or stopping drinking and smoking. These may seem desirable to the missionary or evangelist and there may be some biblical basis for encouraging them, but to make them requirements for baptism would be wrong. The new Christians, feeding on the Word, led by the Holy Spirit, worshiping God in spirit and in truth, will be led to make ethical decisions which for their time and their circumstances are pleasing to God.

More must be said. Often the evangelist or missionary sees some part of the culture as definitely evil, although it is not mentioned in Scripture. Cannibalism is an example. It is the missionary's privilege to help his friends whom he is leading to salvation to renounce this evil aspect of their culture at the same time that they become Christians. One of the castes of India, where a people movement was beginning, used to fine offenders against caste law in bottles of liquor. The greater the offense, the more bottles had to be given to the *punchayat* (the caste council), whose members then proceeded to get drunk together. As groups from this caste became Christian, they kept the *punchayat*; that was a good component of their culture. They renounced the idea that bottles of liquor were a suitable form of punishment; that was a bad component. The wise evangelist or missionary, as he lives and works with groups seriously considering becoming Christian, will lead them to make as many good innovations as he can, without stopping the movement. Educating girls, banning liquor, giving up growing opium, renouncing exorbitant dowries, and many other advances can be instituted, aided by the feeling that "our people are taking a great forward step, of which this is a part." All these are good, yet not one is biblically required. Should requiring some one of them stop the movement, that requirement ought to be dropped.

The third objection is that people movements bring in one-tribe, one-race, one-class congregations. These insure that pride, racism, and exclusiveness continue to mar the Church. There is some substance to this objection. Action taken from prideful notions of racial superiority and with the purpose of excluding other peoples is certainly wrong. Furthermore, one-class, one-race, or one-tribe congregations of a dominant homogeneous unit are in danger of encouraging or at least permitting pride and exclusiveness. This is particularly true in affluent congregations where growth has stopped.

Nevertheless, the Holy Scriptures and the Holy Spirit are so powerfully arrayed against pride and racial exclusiveness that the best way of promoting brotherhood in *non*-Christian segments of society, whether these be classes, tribes, castes, or other homogeneous units, is to multiply Christian congregations among them. Among Christians the tide toward brotherhood is irreversible. Consequently, together with multiplying conglomerate or multiethnic congregations where such action is possible, there ought to go multiplying monoethnic congregations. These automatically keep the door of salvation open to the non-Christians of the class, tribe, or caste concerned. One-by-one conversion out of the social unit wins the individual but loses the people. People movements should be encouraged in order to keep the door to salvation (and gradually more brotherhood) open to as many relatives of the converts as possible. Encouraging them will require significant changes. Momentous decisions will have to be taken by missionaries, nationals, missions, and churches.

The point is so important that I give three illustrations. In Latin America in the 1960s a rapidly growing small denomination of the urban affluent found that when it admitted converts from the poor, that stopped growth from the affluent. Consequently, this denomination retained enough poor members to emphasize that in Christ there is no Jew nor Gentile, no slave nor free, but directed most converts from the poor to other denominations. Had it not done this, it would have slammed shut the door to upper-class converts.

A hundred years ago in Pakistan (then India) a people movement began in the Meg caste. It failed. The story is told in detail by Frederick E. Stock and Margaret A. Stock. They believe that part of the reason for the failure of the Meg movement was that another caste, the Chuhras, started moving to Christian faith in large numbers. Soon "becoming a Christian" meant leaving the Meg caste and joining the Chuhra Church. As the Chuhra movement

gained momentum in the 1880's, Meg baptisms fell off. . . . Megs considered themselves a superior caste to the Chuhras. As a large influx of Chuhras came into the Church, the Megs, who were still hesitating on the brink of decision, were no doubt repelled. Word spread that to become a Christian one must associate closely with those lower on the social scale. This was a serious deterrent.[2]

Muslims in any country, in addition to being of a different religion, are often of a different racial stock from the Christians. For example, in Mindanao, the large southern island in the Philippines, Muslims are the descendants of those tribes which in the 1400s, just before Spain conquered the Philippines, had by people movements espoused Islam. Today for a Muslim in Mindanao to become a Christian would mean as much as for a Lutheran Norwegian to become a Muslim in Albania. The Norwegian would leave his people to become an Albanian. He would eat with Albanians, intermarry with Albanians, and worship with Albanians. If Muslims are to be evangelized effectively, a way must be found for them to become Christian *within their social units*.

The people movement to Christ is that way. It may be the only way. It involves some danger of perpetuating racial exclusiveness; but since conversion to Christianity brings men and women into a faith that teaches and practices brotherhood, the danger must not be exaggerated. It can be overcome. Indeed, if one wants to spread brotherhood, there is no better way than leading great numbers to become Christians. The Bible clearly teaches that all men have one progenitor, Adam; hence, all are brothers and sisters. They all have one Savior, Jesus Christ, and one Book, the Bible. The Bible declares again and again that in Christ all are equal. But if instant brotherhood is demanded as a nonbiblical *prerequisite* for baptism, non-Christian members of the unit being evangelized are beyond question deterred from becoming Christians. To hold to brotherhood as the *goal*, while encouraging monoethnic congregations to arise where this is natural, is intelligent evangelization. It must not be confused with encouraging established Christian congregations and denominations to practice segregation. That is an entirely different thing and is wrong.

The fourth objection is that the people-movement way of evangelization and discipling causes nominality. The truth, of course, is something different—namely, that lack of nurture, possibly in the generation becoming Christian but more likely in their descendants, caused the nominality. Whether Christians come in one by one or group by group, they and their descendants soon become nominal marginal Christians if they are neglected.

2. Frederick E. Stock and Margaret A. Stock, *People Movements in the Punjab* (Pasadena: William Carey Library, 1975), pp. 55–56.

This objection rises in part because as the gathered churches in the west rose out of the state churches, they stressed individual decision. It was commonly said that when the Emperor Constantine became Christian, conversion became easy, and men and women who never intended to lead the Christian life called themselves Christian, accepted baptism, and took their infants to be baptized. This whole process, declared the leaders of the evangelical gathered churches, could not make men Christian. Individual decision was demanded. I write as a member of a denomination which practices believer's baptism. When talking about members of a generally Christianized society becoming personally convinced Christians, I heartily agree with the gathered-church position. In such populations, unless *individuals* consciously accept Jesus Christ as Lord and deliberately intend to obey the Scriptures, taking them in will result in nominalism.

But the people movement is of non-Christian men and women who for the first time are turning to Christian faith. Furthermore, they are turning in a society where to become Christian is held to be betraying one's family and "making another father." Under such circumstances one-by-one evangelization, while it saves the individual (provided he can stand the persecution and outlast the ostracism), *loses the group.* All his relatives are hardened against the gospel. This is precisely where Muslim evangelization is today. The more tightly knit is the homogeneous unit from which the convert comes, the more difficult it is for converts to come one by one. If the Great Commission is to be carried out and *panta ta ethnē* (peoples) are to be discipled, a mode of evangelization must be used which enables converts to remain in their families and kin groups.

It is worth noting that all the followers of our Lord remained in their families. Not one of them felt he was leaving the Jews and becoming a Gentile.

Often today the situation is that the missionary or evangelist would gladly have the convert remain in the family, but the family sternly ostracizes him. Under these circumstances the one-by-one mode of ingathering, although not desired by the evangelist, results. The people movement is God's plan to meet this circumstance. The individual all alone is an easy mark for ostracism, but the group of five, ten, or fifty families is almost impervious to it. Intelligent evangelism, therefore, under such circumstances will encourage people movements to develop. When the missionary preaches or writes tracts, he will give examples of *groups* becoming Christian. He will seldom tell of one person seeking baptism. Group action is the most effective answer to ostracism. True, here and there very strong individuals have accepted Christ and have become outstanding Christians; but only when they have encouraged others of their own people to multi-individual decisions have these strong individuals led many to Christ. In an indifferent or hostile society, one-by-one evangelization closes the door to the intimates and kinfolk of new converts. The people movement enables chains of individuals, group by group, to come to Christ while remaining in their own class, caste, or tribe.

Groups require instruction and Christian nurture; unless they are given, nominality will certainly develop. The way to avoid nominality is to provide adequate nurture.

The fifth objection is that people movements are men's work, whereas true Christianization is the work of the Holy Spirit. To this we reply that people movements must not be understood as men's work. They are the work of the Holy Spirit, as was stated clearly in *The Bridges of God,* which first called attention to how peoples become Christian, and has been repeatedly stated in other writings since then.

When the Spirit of God moves on established congregations and nominal Christians, He produces renewal and revival. God renews divine life that is already there. When He moves on non-Christian societies, *re*vival cannot take place. There must be conversion and a turning of enough men and women so the whole *ethnos* (or segment of society) or a large part of it comes to Christian faith. God desires the salvation of whole peoples. Scripture tells us that the gospel itself was revealed by the command of eternal God precisely to bring *panta ta ethnē,* all the peoples, to obedience of faith (Rom. 16:25–26). As Christians understand people movements, they can cooperate with the Holy Spirit, recognize His work, and make sure that they do not frustrate it by their own indifference and neglect.

Across the ages and in all six continents God Himself has caused most first-time decisions from non-Christian faiths to come by way of people movements. By way of contrast, the one-by-one mode is typical in populations which have already become largely Christian. One-by-one is therefore the mode which most pastors and missionaries know from their own early experience. It brings great growth in "Christian" populations. As renewal movements sweep long-established denominations, whether in Europe, America, Asia, or Africa, most conversions come one by one. But in non-Christian populations, turning for the first time to the Savior, most conversions occur group by group, in

some form of people movement. Thus people movements are necessary at the growing edge of the Church. If the Church would advance
on new ground, she must create and nurture people movements.

To state the same truth in theological language, the Church may
confidently expect God to lead His chosen ones out of Egypt, family by
family, tribe by tribe, class by class, and neighborhood by neighborhood. She ought, therefore, to learn about people movements. She
ought to petition God to breathe on *panta ta ethnē*, that *ethnos* after
ethnos will become Christian. As Bishop V. S. Azariah of Dornakal
wrote in his foreword to *Christ's Way to India's Heart,*

> God alone can touch the hearts of people. The forces that make for
> change of religious allegiance on the part of man are many and often
> beyond human analysis. Such a study as this volume reports [people
> movements] can only be considered as indicating the lines along which
> Christ's followers may intelligently cooperate with Him in accomplish-
> ing His purposes for mankind. It is our duty to watch the movements of
> the Spirit, lest we frustrate God's work by our unbelief, indifference, or
> mismanagement of potential situations. We need divine illumination
> "to have a right judgment on all things."[3]

What does all this mean for ministers, missionaries, and missionary
societies? What momentous decisions are called for so that we do not
frustrate God's work by our own unbelief, indifference, or misman-
agement of potential situations?

Bishop Azariah wrote that sentence because he saw such frus-
tration of God's work constantly going on. Bands of missionaries
and other bands of national Christian leaders were and are quite frequently mismanaging potential group ingatherings. With the best of
intentions they were and are carrying on much good mission work,
which educated Christians, healed the sick, fed the hungry, proclaimed the Word, and did not harvest the ripe grain. All this devoted
labor won a few scores or hundreds of individual converts across the
years and thus planted a few nongrowing congregations but did not
start or further the movement of an entire segment of society to Christ.
Unfortunately, such ineffective mission work is quite common.

Every minister or missionary and every executive of a missionary
society ought therefore to ask himself the following questions. What

---

3. J. Waskom Pickett, *Christ's Way to India's Heart*, 3d ed. (Lucknow: Lucknow Publishing
House, 1960), p. 6.

people groups are in the cities or districts where we work? Which of these are responsive? From which peoples have most of the Christians come? Answering such questions may require a careful survey of the area; but in most cases these questions can be readily answered.

Having found which are the fields ready to harvest, mission leaders should then ask themselves what changes need to be made in order to reap this harvest. Since merely carrying on our present work is not winning this people, what costly decisions must we make to carry out Christ's command that this *ethnos* be discipled—incorporated in His body, the Church? These costly decisions are quite likely to mean turning from good works, which do not start and nurture a people movement to Christ, and beginning the kind of work which does. This will truly be a momentous decision.

For example, while studying a notable piece of mission work in Africa, I came across two "stations" founded and maintained by one missionary society. In the first station the Church in a given seventeen-year period had declined from six thousand to three thousand. In the other during the same period the Church had grown from two thousand to thirty-one thousand. Despite this fact, both stations were occupied by eight missionaries each. Both were carrying on "a fine piece of mission work." The costly decision called for was to transfer six missionaries from station 1 to station 2 or to a new station 3. But the pain and cost involved in such a decision had, until the time of my study, rendered any such action unthinkable. Although this is an unusual example, it well illustrates what costly decisions are likely to mean.

No pastor, no missionary, and no mission executive likes to change a good ongoing work, or to raise significant new money and new workers to engage meaningfully in reaping the ripe fields. But if Christ's command is to be obeyed, such decisions must be made. Group ingathering is truly Christian, truly urgent, and truly Christ's command. To bring it about, new, costly, and often painful decisions are required.

12

Are American Jews a Hidden People?

Today in mission circles one hears a great deal about "hidden" or "unreached" peoples. We have suddenly realized that thousands of whole peoples have very few Christians among them—that is, very few groups of that ethnic unit have ever become Christian. In their area Christians of other segments of society may be numerous; "but to us," a hidden people will say, "Christianity is a foreign religion. Any who become Christians leave *us* and join *them.*"

Consequently, missionaries and missionary societies are now beginning to look for new fields and to ask themselves, "Should we not go on beyond the people or peoples in which, by God's grace, we have planted scores or hundreds of churches, to some of these hidden peoples from whom very few have ever become Christian?" We shall continue to send a few missionaries to help the already established young denomination, but we shall place substantial evangelistic forces in the hidden peoples. We shall take the same step that Philip did when he left the Jerusalem Christians and went to the Samaritans (with whom Jews had no dealings). It seems likely that this concern among dedicated Christians of all continents will continue to mount, for the number of unreached peoples is very great. Some missiologists estimate it at six thousand and some at fifty thousand.

Intelligent action in regard to the hidden peoples requires a clear definition of the words *hidden* and *unreached*. "Hidden" gives the impression of some remote tribe, like the Auca Indians, concealed behind the ranges or in vast swamps. "Unreached" gives the impression that missionaries have not yet gotten that far, or that Christians have not yet established physical contact. In reality, both "hidden" and "unreached" mean something quite different. To clarify the meaning of these words, we lift up one people, the Jews, and ask, "Are they a hidden people?"

As we answer this question, we stress that many hidden peoples live intermingled with Christians. They meet Christians every day and pass the doors of churches frequently. They hear the gospel over the radio and on television. They read about great Christian gatherings in their own nation. But they have not seen that the gospel is *for them*. Hearing, they do not hear. Seeing, they do not perceive. They almost never become Christians.

The Jews are a case in point. In the correct sense of the word, they are a hidden people. They have many Christian neighbors with whom they play golf or visit over the back fence. They invite Christians to their weddings and bar mitzvahs. They are members of many boards and faculties. Nevertheless, they remain a thoroughly hidden people. Very few Jews have become Christians. Mission thinkers (missiologists) must realize that often hidden peoples live among Christians. One may say that a people group is rightly called "hidden" or "unreached" until many of its members become Christian while remaining proudly, unmistakably parts of that people.

Are the Jews a hidden people in this sense? Certainly, because when a Jew "becomes a Christian," in the vast majority of cases he ceases to be a Jew. He ceases to eat kosher, circumcise his boy babies, worship on Saturday, and marry strictly in the Jewish community. When will the Jews become a reached people? When hundreds of thousands of them, after becoming followers of Jesus the Messiah, continue to be Jews and to observe the niceties of Jewish custom. Most particularly they will continue to marry within the Jewish community, holding that for Jewish men there are no better women in the world, none more beautiful, sensible, and companionable than Hebrew maidens.

Moishe Rosen, founder of Jews for Jesus, is one of the few missiological geniuses of our day. In the early sixties he recognized that Jews were hearing the gospel as a proposal to leave "us" and join "them." He invited Jewish people to become—not Christians, heaven forbid!—but *Jews* for Jesus, or Messianic *Jews*, or fulfilled *Jews*.

Operating in the white light which insight casts on the scene, many thousand Jews, perhaps fifty thousand, have become baptized believers in Yeshua Ha Maschiach. Thus they have entered into salvation. They accept the entire Bible as the Word of God. They will rejoice around the throne of God with us and all other believers from every nation, tribe, and tongue.

Rosen recently commented on a letter he had received from a Jewish friend. I quote first from the letter and then from Rosen's revealing comments. Both illustrate the present hiddenness of the Jewish people.

> I was twenty-six years old before I heard the Gospel of salvation through Jesus Christ for the first time; I believed it as soon as I understood it, and submitted my life to Jesus when I was twenty-seven. When I think back on all the preceding years . . . I can only exclaim: "What a waste. Why didn't anyone tell me sooner?"

> Please, never think that we have all heard. The billboards and radio sermons frequently do *not* communicate the Gospel; they merely tell my people that there are a lot of Gentiles around, that we are still a minority. . . . We have heard of the Gentile God Jesus, and the Virgin Mary, but the true meaning of the Gospel has rarely been communicated to *us*. We are a closed community, in that the Jewish teachers, having no understanding of Christianity, misinform us of its meaning; and too many good Christians fear to speak of Jesus to us, lest we be offended. Believe me, being offended is better than being condemned for eternity!

Rosen comments:

> It must seem incredible to you Christians that someone could live in this country for 26 years and never hear the Gospel. Yet most Jews will exit from this life into a Christless eternity never having heard the Good News. Some Christians have the notion that America is already over-evangelized, with more churches, Gospel broadcasts, and evangelistic billboards per capita than any nation in the world. But to the Jew all this only says one thing: "There are a lot of Gentiles around." We Jews are constantly reminded of our minority status. Because all the

Gospel preaching seems to be directed away from the Jews, it seems to us as if the sermons in the churches, the preaching on the t.v. and the radio, and the Jesus billboards are saying "For Gentiles only."

Most Gospel preaching does not take into account that we Jews have been indoctrinated to believe that Christ is for non-Jews only. We've been taught that believing in Jesus makes people hate and persecute us. To this day most Jewish children are told that the Nazi Holocaust was the work of Christians, believers in Jesus who hate us for not accepting their religion and for "killing" their God. We Jews are led to believe that it is the courageous thing, the Jewish thing, the necessary thing NOT TO LISTEN when Christians try to tell us of their religion which is the worship of a dead Jew. We have seen too many Jews killed already on account of the Gentile religion of Christianity. The only loyal thing to do is to refuse to listen.

Most of my fellow Jews have never heard that Jesus Christ died for *their* sins as well as the sins of the whole world, that He rose again and brings new life to Jews and Gentiles alike. And that believing in Him causes people to love one another. Yes, we want to tell our fellow Jews that there are non-Jews who love our people, that believing in Jesus in a biblical way CAUSES PEOPLE TO LOVE, NOT HATE.

There are growing numbers of Jews like us who have discovered the true meaning of the Christian life. As we take our place in the church, we find that our fellow Christians want to HONOR our Jewish heritage. The notion with which we have been indoctrinated is false. Yet the false notion of "cultural and ethnic genocide committed by preaching the Gospel" is still the filter through which the Jewish mind comprehends the message of Jesus. It is the fabric of the veil which clouds the vision of the people of Israel today.

As long as that attitude prevails, the Jews will remain a thoroughly hidden people even while living among other Americans.

Hundreds of other segments of mankind are also hidden. Their members rub shoulders with Christians. They have many friends among Christians. They work together and play together with Christians. But very few of them become Christ's disciples. Muslims as a whole, no matter where they live and how many Christians they know, are hidden people. The nearly three thousand separate endogamous castes in India—six hundred million individuals—are three thousand hidden peoples. Until quite recently the Maasai in Kenya, surrounded by Christian tribes, remained a hidden people. "None of us become Christians," they thought.

A missionary to Rwanda wrote in April 1982,

> The Twa here are an unreached people, hidden from the eyes of the churches and missionaries. The Hutu and the Tutsi consider the Twa animalistic and question their ability to comprehend the Gospel. The existing churches will not reach out to the Twa. Evangelizing them will take a special effort, unrelated to existing churches.

The highly secularized sections of university faculties in America constitute a hidden people, although they work closely with Christians on the same faculties. The Marxist sections of most nations are another modern form of hidden peoples. Whether in America or Africa or any other continent, hidden peoples often exist with Christians, yet effectively hidden from them.

As the attention of the Christian world turns to unreached peoples, it is of the greatest importance to realize that the task is to press on beyond those people groups from which many have become Christian. In these, men and women can become Christian without leaving their own folk.

The task is to disciple enough individuals and groups of *each* hidden people so that its members recognize that "one of us can become a follower of Christ *while remaining thoroughly one of us.*"

As missionary societies plan for the future, they should take seriously the references to the *ethnē* in the Great Commission and many other New Testament passages. The inspired writers of the revelation of God do not use the Greek word *ethnē* carelessly. Christians cannot say, "Romans 16:25–26 says that the gospel was revealed to bring all the peoples *(ethnē)* of the world to faith and obedience, but Paul could have used the word *individuals* just as well." It is the unswerving purpose of God that all the *peoples* of earth, all the *ethnē*, be brought to faith and obedience as separate *ethnē*. That is why the gospel was revealed.

Missionary societies should think in terms of discipling *ethnos* after *ethnos* until *panta ta ethnē* have been discipled. Missions should survey each field to see where the most receptive people is, and then concentrate enough laborers there to get a Christward movement flowing within that people. Christianization should preserve a people, heighten its sense of peoplehood, and increase its ethnic identity. To become a Christian must cease to mean "leaving my people" and come to mean "pioneering a better way for my people." As this happens, then, one by one, hidden peoples will become discipled peoples. That is the task of missions. That is what missiology is all about.

13

Asians in Britain

A million Asians live in Britain. They are typical of many minorities in America and other lands. A brief look at the opportunities and problems of their evangelization will be illuminating. Evangelizing them will require momentous decisions.

1. *Christians blind themselves when they speak of "the Asian million" as if it were a single block.* The million consist of at least a dozen kinds of Asians—linguistic groups, Hindus, Muslims, Sikhs, Secularists, and materialists. Some are educated, some are not. Sri Lankans, Pakistanis, Indians, Singaporeans, and others form tight communities, which hold other groups of Asians at almost as much distance as they do white Britons.

2. *If the million are invited to join either white or Asian congregations of ethnic units other than their own, the response will be minimal.* If the invitation to "come unto me, all you who labor" is to be accepted, it must be heard as an invitation to remain oneself linguistically and ethnically while following the Lord Jesus. In the New Testament church the greatest growth took place when Jews joined Jewish congregations, Samaritans joined Samaritan congregations, and Cornelius's congregation continued to meet in Colonel Cornelius's distinctly Italian patio. The Holy Spirit fell on Cornelius and his household where Peter and his companions were the only Jews among perhaps fifty Italians.

3. *Christ does certainly call to unity, and we affirm that in Christ there is no Jew nor Greek; however, we must also affirm ethnicity.* The New Testament congregations were strikingly monoethnic. Indeed, the Jewish churches described in the first few chapters of Acts were not only 100 percent Jewish; they were also strikingly congregations of common people. Very few Pharisees, Sadducees, rulers of the people, or scribes joined the congregations.

4. *Christianity must hold these two forces in equal tension.* We must not espouse only one of them. Unity must be a goal. So must ethnic diversity. Christ did not come to destroy *panta ta ethnē,* but to disciple them. Revelation tells us that before the throne will be people from all the ethnic units and languages of Planet Earth. Their languages and ethnic distinctions will remain intact until the end.

The facts about Asians in Britain are set forth by V. M. Kattapuram in the April 1980 issue of *Outreach,* published by India Evangelical Mission. He says that the two thousand Christians among the million Asians are also divided by origin, language, and denomination. The two Syrian Christian congregations in Britain remain distinctly Syrian. They worship in Malayalam, and they marry only Syrian Christians. They do not invite Muslims or Gujerati-speaking Indians to join their congregations. This is perfectly natural—a normal outcome of the fact that Christianity flows best within each ethnic unit, within each linguistic unit.

5. *Because the battle for brotherhood is raging so strongly and Christians are making such heroic efforts to overcome ethnic pride, any recognition of ethnicity meets with considerable and sometimes fierce opposition.* "Any stress on ethnicity," such Christians shout, "is segregation and racial pride. Down with it." These shouts are understandable but mistaken. Down with racism; yes. Down with ethnic pride and exclusiveness; yes. Down with the oppression of subject peoples; yes. All Christians agree. There is no argument here.

6. *There should be equal agreement on the fact that the faith flows most naturally and fastest along ethnic and linguistic lines.* An English-speaking congregation which invited French-speaking people to join it would meet with very limited success. In New Testament times, if Samaritan congregations had invited Jews to join their congregations, they would have met with chilly refusal. The best and perhaps the most effective way to break down racism and castism is to lead each people, each class, each segment of the total population to become disciples of the Lord Jesus. Then they will realize that all are

children of Adam and hence brothers and sisters; all are equally sinners, and believers are equally saved. Anything that hinders enrollment of the segments of the Asian population in Britain keeps brotherhood from spreading. Intelligent mission will proceed on ethnic lines.

7. *Where true melting pots have developed, where urbanization or famine and the sword have actually broken down ethnic distinctions, there evangelism will prosper when and if it announces that Christians are one new people.* But true melting pots are rare. Most melting pots on examination turn out to be stew pots, in which meat remains meat, and carrots remain carrots, all slightly flavored by the mix. We must not insist that melting-pot evangelism is the only true evangelism. It is one form of evangelism. But it is neither the only biblical form nor the most effective.

In conclusion, if the Asian mosaic in Britain is to be evangelized effectively, it must be approached in view of the ethnic realities. Muslim Pakistanis are not going to join Syrian churches speaking Malayalam—nor will the Syrian churches invite them to do so. Gujerati merchant-caste people in London are not going to join congregations made up of Trinidadian Christians, who are descendants of low-caste indentured laborers from South India and determined to maintain in their congregations a Trinidadian culture and dominance.

We have been speaking about one million souls merely to illustrate a universal principle. Mankind everywhere, like Asians in Britain, exists as a mosaic of multitudinous pieces. Effective evangelization of the twenty-five million Hispanics in North America must see that block as a mosaic, and must evangelize each piece of the mosaic in a way particularly suited to it. Each part must be brought into congregations where the deacons, elders, pastors, and leaders are members of that section. The Chinese in Hong Kong or Singapore are also composed of many quite distinct linguistic and ethnic units. Guatemalans are in reality a cluster of scores of distinct segments of mankind.

The sovereign Lord is commanding advance. He intends a vast liberation of men and women into the freedom of Christ. But to be effective, this message of redemption and freedom must be heard and understood. The invitation is not to join European congregations, speaking English, nor for the highly educated to join congregations of illiterates, nor for factory workers to join congregations dominated by college students and their teachers. The message of redemption must invite those who hear and believe to form congregations where they feel at home and enjoy normal, easy, and loving relationships with the rest of the congregation. Brotherhood will come. Make no mistake, the Lord God Almighty will bring it. Bible-believing and obeying Christians will institute it. But to give the spirit of love and brotherhood the greatest chance, it must flow through congregations of like-cultured people.

Bright days and great victories lie ahead—if only we hold steadily in mind Christ's command to disciple whole segments of society, whole *ethnē*, whole castes and tribes and peoples.

14

A Necessary Innovation: International Teams

Many western nations, having become highly secularized and feeling quite secure as to their position in the world, grant visas freely to missionaries of any religion—Hinduism, Buddhism, Islam, Marxism, theosophy, or the minor sects of each. Third-world countries, on the contrary, grant visas grudgingly. They feel they must avoid domination by the west. They believe that their national *ethos* is bound up with their ancestral religion. Even Hindu India, which proudly claims that it is exceedingly tolerant toward all forms of religion (they all lead toward God), commonly denies visas to those who advocate Christianity.

As a result, third-world nations grant visas to missionaries with increasing reluctance. Unless the developed nations begin demanding reciprocity, obtaining visas will become more and more difficult. Were the United States Congress to pass a law that it would grant visas to Hindu missionaries only if India would freely grant visas to American missionaries, the situation might change. However, such action by Congress or other governments of developed nations does not seem likely. Rather it looks as if visas to western missionaries will grow more and more difficult to obtain.

121

Reaching the Unreached: Two Possible Answers

How then are the unreached peoples to be won to Christ? How are we to evangelize the three billion men and women in whose segments of society very few have ever become Christian? Two answers are commonly given.

Some people suggest that we let the national churches do it. The Church of Jesus Christ now exists in practically every nation in the world. The day of sending missionaries is over. Mission from now on is each congregation and denomination carrying on mission in its own neighborhood.

This answer can be given only by those who do not know the situation or who do not believe that God commands that the gospel be made known to all segments of society in every nation-state on earth. Knowledgeable Christians, however, cannot possibly give that answer. They are painfully aware that more than half of earth's people are not hearing the gospel at all. Informed Christians know that national Churches, in which are less than 1 percent of a nation's population and whose members are frequently illiterate and desperately poor, cannot possibly evangelize 5 percent of their compatriots and will usually do very well if they evangelize .1 percent. The sixty-thousand-member Lutheran Church in Tamil Nadu, India, for example, most of whose members have come from the depressed classes, cannot possibly evangelize the forty million Hindus who belong to hundreds of respectable castes in that populous state. The Lutheran Church will do very well indeed if it adds ten thousand converts from Hinduism to its membership in the next ten years.

Those who intend to obey Christ and evangelize all the *ethnē* of the world must not take refuge in rosy dreams, imagining that new and often weak denominations in Asia, Africa, and Latin America will or can complete the huge task of world evangelization. Christians obeying God's command to evangelize the world must deal honestly with hard realities.

Others offer a second answer: In this new day, the denominations of Asia, Africa, and Latin America are greatly expanding what they have been doing. They are organizing missionary societies which intend to reach the unreached, to obey the Great Commission, to evangelize segments of mankind in which are few if any Christians. Let us thank God for these societies and cooperate with them. They and we are "partners in obedience."

The word *cooperate* has many meanings. Often it means, "Let western denominations and missionary societies provide the money and nonwestern societies the men." At other times it means, "Let us decide together where to work." Sometimes it means no more than "Let us once a year have a meeting of missionaries from all missions operating in this area and encourage one another." Many other meanings are assigned to that useful word *cooperate*.

The thousands of nationals working to spread the gospel among the three billion are certainly a positive factor in world evangelization. Every new missionary society from any nation-state in any continent is a cause for rejoicing. It is a step in the right direction. How big a step is it? That depends entirely on how effective it is. How many men and women has it led to Christ? How many new churches has it planted? Is it establishing self-supporting congregations and denominations? Or is the new missionary society strictly a seed-sowing operation?

Furthermore, does "cooperation" aid multiplying sound ongoing congregations? Or is it merely an occasion for friendly intercourse between sister missions? Much cooperation results in no observable growth in any of the churches concerned. Conversely, some of the most effective missionary work has been done by notably *un*cooperative missions. The Roman Catholic missions are notably *un*cooperative with Protestant missions—and in many lands are highly successful in carrying out the Great Commission. The tremendous growth of Baptist churches in east Andhra was not achieved in close cooperation with Anglican and Lutheran missions working there.

In short, whatever cooperation with third-world missionary societies means, it must be welcomed; at the same time it must be recognized as only a small step in the right direction. Partnership in obedience is sometimes a means to the end (effective evangelization), but it is never an idol to be worshiped.

Reaching the Unreached: An Innovative Answer

With this as background we ask, "How is world evangelization to be carried out when only a few visas are granted to missionaries from the developed nations?" We answer, "By making missionary teams international."

Mission executives, missiologists, and leaders of churches should note an article in the December 1981, *Omnis Terra,* published by the Pontifical Missionary Union of Rome. The article is titled "Divine Word

Missionaries are Eighty-Four Percent Indians." *There* is the urgently needed innovation. Instead of missionary teams being made up exclusively of the sons and daughters of the sending land, often they may to advantage be made up 84 percent of the citizens of the receiving land and 16 percent of the citizens of the sending land. Proportions will vary. They may be six to one, three to one, or one to one.

Forming the Missionary Teams

Such missionary teams will be funded by missionary-minded Christians banded together in societies in one country and sent into the harvest in some other country. We should carefully note God's word to us:

> "Behold, days are coming," declares the Lord GOD,
> "When I will send a famine on the land,
> Not a famine for bread or a thirst for water,
> But rather for hearing the words of the LORD." [Amos 8:11]

When millions are dying in a great famine of the Word of God, it is urgent to distribute the bread of heaven. Whether workers are Chinese, Korean, German, American, or Indian is a secondary consideration.

Someone will instantly object, saying that the Church in each land must support its own pastors and leaders. Creating subsidized dependent congregations and denominations is a bankrupt mission policy. We used to do that, and it has again and again proved erroneous.

The objection is easily answered. The innovation being proposed is not (repeat, not) to pay national pastors with American or European money. It is to deploy nationals as missionaries who will work ahead of the Church, in segments of the population from which practically no one has become Christian. As congregations are established in that population, they will, of course, support their own pastors. The national missionaries of one segment of the population will not become pastors of the churches they founded in some other segment. Like missionaries in the past, chiefly Americans and Europeans, they will win converts, father people movements, multiply congregations, and then move on. The missionary team is there only temporarily. It will go on and leave the self-supporting congregations to be led by their own sons. A subsidized dependent denomination will not be created.

Organizing the Work

Obviously all members of the missionary team would have to learn thoroughly the language of the people among whom they would be proclaiming Christ. All would receive at least a year of education in the history of missions, missionary methods, the science of communication, the study of other religions with the purpose of presenting Christ effectively to their adherents, and other useful missionary studies. Raising money in the sending congregations would be the work of the sons and daughters of those congregations.

This innovation requires work *beyond* the existing Church. A different people would be evangelized. The scene of labors would usually be a district two hundred or more miles away from the national Church. Consequently, administration would be a burden carried by the team itself. The existing national Church would not assume the burden of administering the missionary team. The national Church would usually be asked for its blessing. Sons of some national Church would be enrolled as missionaries in the team but would follow team rules, not church rules.

For example, in 1979 the World Literature Crusade (WLC) of California sent almost ten million dollars abroad to distribute Gospels and tracts in many lands. In that year it also employed more than one thousand Indian workers in India. They were trained, deployed, and directed by fifteen highly trained Indians. All were paid on Indian standards. Those of the one thousand workers who did a fine job were retained. Those who did not carry out the purposes of the WLC were discharged. As a result a Gospel or a tract was actually put into practically every home in the eight-hundred thousand villages and towns of India. The task force was Indian. The supporting funds were entirely American. The missionary impact on India was impressive.

Summarizing the Program

Missionary-minded Christians will organize and finance missionary teams consisting in part of their own sons and daughters, who will need visas, and in part of the nationals of the nation-state being evangelized.

The missionaries, both foreign and national, will not work in the tribes, castes, clans, or segments of society which already have been discipled. They will work among unreached peoples.

These missionary teams will administer themselves according to the principles laid down by their sending societies. The burden of administration will not rest on the young Churches or missionary societies of the country in which work is being carried on, although, of course, the most cordial relationships will be maintained. Those young Churches and missionary societies will no doubt give their blessings to the teams.

Since many of the sons and daughters of the younger Church will be employed by and be a part of the missionary team, a mutually agreeable relationship can be assumed. The discipling of a new segment of society, beyond the existing Churches, must not be loaded onto them. It is a new enterprise, in which both the missionary society, which organized the team, and Churches, in whose country it works, will praise God for it; but only those who carry the financial burden will administer it.

For example, assume that the Nairs of Kerala, South India, are to be evangelized. Mar Thoma, Orthodox, Roman Catholic Syrian, or Church of South India congregations are found near most Nair communities; but to date none of these congregations has carried on a sustained program to disciple Nairs and multiply Nair churches. The missionary team beginning Nair evangelization would consist of ten Americans and ninety Naga Christians from northeast India. Let us further assume that the inspiration and funding for this team come entirely from America.

The Nairs in the southwest tip of India will be evangelized by the team of Americans and Naga Christians. There will be no Nairs on the missionary team proclaiming the gospel to them. As Nair congregations are established, however, all the elders and pastors will be Nairs. None will be Naga or American. As soon as the Nair congregations are numerous and biblical enough, the missionary team will move on to some other unreached people. Then some of its missionaries might be Nairs.

For a second example, we turn to West Malaysia. Let us assume that the eight hundred thousand Tamil-speaking workers on the rubber plantations in West Malaysia are the receptive segment of society being discipled; the missionary team is made up of two Korean missionaries and eighteen Hindi-speaking missionaries from north India; and the dream of such a team and its funding come entirely from Korea. Its administration would be carried on by the team itself with constant reference to the Korean missionary society which was raising the funds for this large enterprise. No existing national Church in West Malaysia would feel responsible for or direct the enterprise. All existing Churches would, however, rejoice in this great new resource for the spread of the gospel in their land. The relationship of existing national Churches to those new missions would be precisely the relationship of the Methodist Church of South Asia to a new Pentecostal or Roman Catholic mission which moved into a neighboring district to disciple a responsive population there.

As this urgently needed innovation goes into effect around the world, warm-hearted members of existing denominations in every country will wake to the glory and urgency of discipling *panta ta ethnē*. They will then organize their own missionary societies (in Namibia as well as New England) and send out their own international missionary teams, which will step up their efficiency by adding to themselves citizens of other lands acceptable in the nation to which the team goes.

Since China is friendly to Pakistan, a team made up of one American and twenty Pakistani Christians might be admitted to work in the extreme west of China, where the paved road from Pakistan emerges from the mountains onto the tableland of far west Sinkiang. The innovation we are proposing would encourage such action.

As long as three billion men and women have yet to believe, there is abundant work for all. As long as the unreached peoples of the world number twenty-six thousand or by other counts fifty-six thousand separate *peoples* (castes, tribes, segments of society), no one need fear that this innovation will damage the initiative of the national Churches. They can praise God and stream ahead with as much of their own missionary work as they can possibly do.

Today sees world evangelization being carried out by thousands of missionary societies, denominations (Churches), and dedicated individuals. There are many methods. In this complex world God blesses many ways of telling the Good News and encouraging men and women to believe on the Savior. God calls many kinds of teams and sends them to do His bidding. We propose international teams not as the one and only right method, but rather as one good method. When the task can be done best by an international team, let each missionary society working there make the momentous decision to organize and send out such a team.

Part 3

Momentous Decisions about Missionary Societies

15

Unchain Missionary Societies

Contrary to the common promotional picture, the missionary movement in far too many places has ground to a halt. Mainline Churches are sending few missionaries. Evangelical Churches are sending more. But both mainline and evangelical Churches and missionary societies tell their workers:

> We send you to do what the national Church tells you. As long as it wants you, we will support you. You must do what it directs. It is in charge. The initiative is totally with the national Church, not with us. The days of paternalistic colonial missions are over. Do you understand?

In short, the missionary society, in this new day, happily agrees to being chained to existing work, to established Churches.

The Limitations of National Churches

Under these circumstances the number of missionaries sent out usually declines. Even when it increases, instead of going out to evangelize the "yet to believe," missionaries go "to help the national Church." That is held to be today's missionary task. Some national Churches are carrying on effective evangelism and multiplying churches in unreached segments of society. Unfortunately, many—

131

and possibly most—national Churches are doing very little to evangelize the unreached *ethnoses* which together make up three billion souls. For the most part the national Church is looking after itself, educating men in seminaries to be pastors of existing congregations, solving its internal problems, and trying to meet pressing financial demands. It talks about evangelism, and (if World Vision or some other organization calls a great pastors' conference and pays the way of pastors to it) assembles for a week or more of inspiration and "evangelism"; but it does little by way of discipling the many untouched and unreached segments of society.

The new missionary movements of the national churches are a bright spot, of course; but they do not reach 5 percent of the three billion.

Most missionary societies in the west (even conservative evangelical missionary societies) have felt the impact of this unforeseen and unfortunate blockage of today's missionary task. It is, of course, right to honor national churches, and in the populations in which they are really evangelizing non-Christians effectively, to leave the task to them or to help them do it. There is no debate at that point. But in the enormous numbers of whole peoples which they are not evangelizing and cannot evangelize, the missionary societies of the world must not remain chained. The total initiative must not be loaded onto already burdened national Churches.

Recently Moishe Rosen, the insightful executive of Jews for Jesus, had his missionary plans turned around by leaders of national Churches. The sad story is well worth telling.

Rosen, whose new approach to Jews is proving effective in America, began to feel that Jews for Jesus ought to send missionaries to Israel. Unfortunately, he decided to go to Israel and consult the national Churches. He talked to many leaders of many branches of the Church. All said to him, "You ought not to send missionaries from America to us. We can do the job far better than your missionaries. Send us the money. We will do the job. In these days, citizens of the land must propagate the gospel. There are quite a number of us Christians here. Leave the job to us."

As a result, Jews for Jesus did not send American missionaries to Israel. Its unique and valuable insight that Hebrew men and women can and ought to become not Christians—heaven forbid!—but Jews for Jesus, followers of Yeshua Ha Maschiach, was not implemented. Jews for Jesus in the state of Israel would have been intensely patriotic, ardent citizens of Israel advocating that the land not be called the West Bank but be called Judea. Such followers of our Lord would commend Christ in Israel far more effectively than traditional Christians.

Rosen's experience is descriptive of a far larger reality than Israel. This sad story, considerably amplified, is uncomfortably like what many leaders of national Churches in many lands are saying about missionaries from abroad. The parallels are painful. The fact is that leaders of Churches in the third world and in the first world too usually feel that missionaries from the outside are likely to damage the Christian cause. Missionaries elicit angry reactions from non-Christians, whose attitudes resemble those of American Christians toward the Moonies and Hare Krishna people. In addition, the missionary cause is now experiencing the anger of African, Asian, and Latin American Christian leaders who (sometimes understandably) resent missionaries. "If they come," such leaders say, "they must ask our permission first and must do what we tell them to do." All the while the three billion who have yet to hear are growing to be four billion! The number of missionaries sent by the younger Churches is increasing—perhaps fifteen thousand by 1985; but the enormous masses of the unreached bear eloquent testimony that more and more missionaries are needed to actively work in unreached populations in which there is no church.

A Solution to the Problem

I have been writing as if the missionary task in every place were the same. Of course, it is not. The missionary task, the task of world evangelization, the discipling of the nations, has tens of thousands of pieces, each one different. When this is recognized, the problem is well on the way to solution.

The science of missiology and the missionary societies of every nation—Korea as well as Kansas, Brazil as well as Belgium—need to remember the following five facts.

1. *In vast populations the national denominations are not reaching and cannot reach 5 percent of the "yet to believe."* True, some national churches in some favored lands facing highly receptive populations are doing most effective evangelization; but in many nations and regions of the globe the younger Churches are growing very slowly, are static, or are declining.

2. *Many more missionaries are needed today.* More will be needed tomorrow, when the world's population will be 6 billion, of whom in 1999 at least 4.5 billion will not yet believe on Christ.

The fact that missionaries make mistakes must not be allowed to obscure this need and diminish the number of ambassadors of Christ. Sometimes they may do the task less well than some trained nationals who are working at the task, but the number of national Christians working effectively at discipling non-Christians is small. Most pastors abroad, like most pastors at home, spend most of the time with the already saved. They do not vigorously evangelize men and women of other segments of society, other peoples, in other languages.

3. *The missionary task is precisely to evangelize those whom national Churches have not evangelized, who have yet to hear and yet to believe.* Part of the problem is caused by missionaries who spend most of their time with the existing Church teaching in seminaries, leading Bible-study classes for pastors (in English), or in other ways serving the national Church.

4. *A sharp distinction must be made between the opinions of two groups of nationals.* The first group is younger Church leaders who are doing little or nothing at all by way of proclaiming Christ to the lost; the second, younger Church leaders who are putting in much time reaching the unreached and are winning converts. The first can be counted on not to want missionaries. Their opinions ought to be disregarded. The opinion of the second group ought to be carefully studied.

5. *It is imperative that mission thinkers differentiate among three classes of populations.*

Non-Christian segments of society now being effectively evangelized by national pastors and laymen.

Non-Christian peoples *not* being evangelized but who live intermingled with existing Christians (e.g., Jews in California, factory laborers in Hong Kong, respectable castes in India).

Non-Christian people groups not or only slightly intermingled with Christians.

Missionaries ought not to evangelize class 1. It is already being evangelized effectively. Converts are being won by national Churches.

Missionaries should evangelize class 2. National Churches may be able to help in this task; or, if they are already doing a little, the missionary may help them do more.

In class 3, missionaries ought to work quite independently of the national Churches, whose blessing (but not management) might be sought. The onerous task of managing the enterprise should not be loaded onto the Churches. Christian denominations and congregations in Calcutta, for example, are not evangelizing the one hundred thousand Satnamis, the two hundred thousand Kayasths, or three hundred or more other unreached castes living there. Missionaries from Korea or America have no moral duty to ask permission of any Indian denomination to evangelize these unreached peoples in Calcutta, although of course cordial relations with these churches would be established.

World evangelization and the discipling of all peoples is so clearly Christ's will, the task has so many facets, and today's technological advances are so numerous that unchaining missionary societies is urgent. These missionary societies must be free to proclaim Christ and disciple the nations in any way they can devise. Existing churches in California, for example, must not object in the slightest degree to Korean churches sending Korean missionaries to multiply churches among the unchurched in California. Rather they should welcome them.

Western missionary societies should not limit themselves to sending Americans or Europeans as missionaries. For example, some innovative American society ought to recruit fifty earnest Javanese Christians who twenty years ago were Muslims, train them thoroughly (possibly for two or three years), and send them to evangelize some segment of the Muslim world. Suppose ten fine Indonesian Christians (formerly Muslims) were to be thoroughly trained and sent by an American missionary society to the three hundred thousand Muslims in the eastern fringe of Zaire or to the million or so Muslims in the western end of Mindanao (the huge southernmost island in the Philippines), or indeed to the one hundred thousand Muslims now living in Detroit or London. Such missionaries ought to be effective communicators of the gospel. If it were helpful, they could be accompanied by missionaries with a Muslim background from Pakistan, Great Britain, America, or Egypt. The international character of the missionary movement needs to be exhibited far more than it is today. In Christ we are all one; there is no Jew nor Greek, no Javanese, American, or Norwegian. Let the missionary movement fly the flag of one world, one race, one gospel.

Executives managing missionary societies and raising the money to carry on the work will say, "All this will require new funds and new donors. Existing donors are giving to existing works. Reaching the three billion will require great new convictions backed by unceasing prayer. Only then will the missionaries and the money for these new tasks be forthcoming."

This is accurate. Unchained missionary societies will immediately set about two urgent tasks. First, they will create a conscience on mission. Just as William Carey had to create among British Christians a conscience on evangelizing India, so mission executives of today will have to create a conscience concerning the four billion unreached who in 1990 will populate the earth. Unchaining missionary societies means convincing millions of Christians of the urgency of frontier mission.

Second, unchaining missionary societies also means discerning and describing the evangelistic problems and opportunities which mark each one of the tens of thousands of unreached segments of society. Not only must the missionary society arouse a conscience that each *ethnos* must be evangelized (discipled), but also it must understand the unique problems which up to the present time have kept that *ethnos* from being discipled, and the unique opportunities which that particular *ethnos* brings.

What this second task means will differ for every piece of the mosaic. One illustration, which concerns six hundred million people, will illustrate both the problems and the opportunities.

In India in 1984 are about twenty-four million Christians. Four million of them are Syrian Christians (Roman Catholic, Orthodox, and Mar Thoma), and twenty million are overwhelmingly from the former untouchable castes and aboriginal tribes. From only 21 tribes and castes have significant numbers become Christian. From another 50 low castes a few hundred or a thousand or two have become Christian. We thus may say that from only 71 of the more than 3,000 castes in India have any sizable numbers become Christians. That means that from 2,929 castes very, very few have become Christian. The few who have done so have been promptly ostracized, outcasted, and declared dead by their caste fellows.

In consequence, the church in India, both Roman Catholic and Protestant, is widely regarded by the six hundred million of the respectable castes as a very low-caste organization. In addition, its members eat meat, even beef! Consequently, even if respectable-caste Hindus hear the gospel, read the Bible, and come to believe on Jesus Christ, they do not become practicing members of existing churches.

All evangelistic efforts by existing congregations and denominations of necessity say, "Believe on Jesus Christ and become members of our congregations." As a result, very, very few respectable-caste Hindus accept baptism and join existing churches.

As long as Christian missions from outside India (from Korea, the Philippines, Brazil, or Europe and North America) regard their work as exclusively aiding the younger churches, they are perceived as inviting believers from the castes to join existing churches. This, of necessity, effectively prohibits respectable-caste inquirers from becoming confessed, baptized, practicing followers of the Savior.

It is at this precise point, facing this precise problem and this precise opportunity, that unchaining missionary societies working in the vast subcontinent of India becomes crucial.

Missionary societies from outside India and Christian broadcasters from outside India have a unique opportunity. They can invite respectable-caste Indians to renounce all idols and other scriptures, to believe on Jesus Christ as God and only Savior, and to become members of His Body, the Church, in groups of men and women from their own neighborhoods, of their own level in society, and of their own educational and financial status.

When we see the tremendous multiplication of house churches which has taken place in mainland China, we are encouraged to believe that a similar multiplication could take place in India. In mainland China the existing churches (Three-Self Churches) planted by missionaries in the nineteenth and early twentieth centuries have been most critical of the congregations which were formed outside the orbits of the Three-Self congregations. It is to be hoped that the existing Churches in India (Baptist, Lutheran, Episcopalian, and Roman Catholic) will be much more friendly to the multiplication of house churches in neighborhoods and among people presently unreached by the existing Churches. It is to be hoped that they will recognize that unless they themselves start multiplying churches among the respectable castes, it is clearly God's will that such churches be started by broadcasters from other lands.

In the light of this one example it is clear that the problems and opportunities which face missionary societies working beyond the existing younger Churches are numerous. The one example which is given merely illustrates a widespread situation. Different problems and different opportunities exist in each country. Those existing in Germany, Scotland, Australia, or California will be quite different from that which I have just described. The principle, however, remains the same. If the national churches concerned are not able to reap, evangelism from outside must wield the sickle. Missionary societies must be unchained. That means, to be sure, work in cordial relationships with the churches (large or small) in the area. That means, even more importantly, they must reach the unreached, find the lost, and multiply churches in every segment of society.

Momentous decisions as to the use of time and money will be involved.

In conclusion, the rightful honoring of the younger Churches, the correct desire that they be masters in their own houses, must not be allowed to reduce the missionary task to the small though necessary duty of assisting national Churches. Unchain the missionary societies of every land. Send missionaries to the three billion who have yet to believe the gospel. In obedience to the Great Commission, disciple the hundred thousand or more segments of mankind (*ethnē*) from which very few have ever become Christian. Enroll millions as committed Christians. Christ commands it.

16

The Revolution in Mission

A revolution has taken place in mission, as understood by the leadership at Geneva and all over the world. Both the ends and the means of new mission are different. The vast machinery of mission is being turned quietly in a new direction to the service of a new theology.

Classical mission has been the presentation of Christ to those who do not believe on Him, with the purpose of leading them to believe and become new creatures in Him and dependable members of His Body, the Church. New mission is everything that the Churches or that Christians ought to do outside their four walls. A plethora of definitions is found, of which the following ten are samples:

1. The Church exists to bring the love of God to the world and in so doing to bring the world to the God of love (p. 1).
2. To share in Christ's mission is to let the world overhear our praises (p. 1).
3. The mission of the Church is the same all over the world (p. 3).
4. Mission is not the kindness of the lucky to the unlucky; it is mutual united obedience to the one God whose mission it is (p. 12).
5. Mission is the extension of the love of God to people, not only by preaching but also by practical Christian service (p. 27).

139

6. Mission is engagement with the local community and its decision centres (p. 55).

7. Mission is assisting the Church in each land to witness to Christ as already present and active in its religious and social and political ferment, to respond to Him there, and to acknowledge Him as the source and goal of their . . . life (p. 68).

8. The mission of the Church is to make its specially Christian contribution to the ongoing educational life of the nation (p. 111).

9. Mission closes the gap between the Church and the laboring sections of European society (p. 15).

10. Mission speaks about human need where it is closest to the bone and influences decisions so that personal relationships are formed in an atmosphere of trust instead of hatred and rivalry (p. 16).[1]

These definitions of mission are a fair sample. This is the sort of thing that "new mission" feels called of God to do. Although occasionally the proclamation of the gospel and the winning of men to personal faith in Christ seem to be at least part of the goal, mission is defined mostly as if it were everything the Christian should do, except lead men to become disciples of Christ.

Part of this is, no doubt, because writers and speakers erroneously assume that at present all missions are already spending all their efforts in persuading men to accept Jesus Christ as Lord and Savior and that a strong case must be made for churches everywhere doing their Christian duty to their neighbors and to society in general. Barry Till, for example, speaking to Anglicans in *Changing Frontiers in the Mission of the Church,* says, "Before the Church of England can join in the MRI programme of advance, we have to continue to meet our present overseas commitments. . . . [These amount to] some two thousand missionaries and sending about two million pounds overseas annually."[2]

However, only a very small portion of the overseas commitments of most denominations goes to propagating the gospel among unbelievers. A large part goes to nation-building activities and to

1. Barry Till, ed., *Changing Frontiers in the Mission of the Church* (London: S.P.C.K., 1965).
2. Ibid., p. 10.

assisting existing Churches. The real danger is not that too much of the Church's effort will be spent in evangelism, but that far too little of it will be.

Let there be no mistake. Human need is complex. Humanity is oppressed by many foes. The battle must be pressed against racism in all its forms, poverty, sickness and malnutrition, the reckless multiplication of births which neutralizes every advance, and the injustice inherent in wealthy nations growing wealthier and poor nations growing poorer. All this is granted; but in no period of history are these the only battles. In view of the small efforts being put forth by many missionary societies to proclaim the gospel to the myriad unreached peoples and to win them to Christ, these other activities must not supplant discipling. The small percentage of missionaries and the small share of church funds now being spent to win the three billion to Christ must not get smaller with the years. It must rapidly grow larger.

At the 1968 meeting of the World Council of Churches at Uppsala, the Division of World Mission and Evangelism deliberately omitted any reference to conversion mission in its program for the next decade. The one sentence which now occupies a prominent place in subsection 2 of the statement was inserted only after the Norwegian delegation threatened to withdraw from the plenary session if any mention of evangelism was omitted. The document was then sent back for redrafting. Omitting all references to evangelism is exactly what we protest. Responsible church leaders of every denomination in the world should cheerfully give the most important place in all their pronouncements to the winning of men to Christ. Of course, an important place must be given to remaking families, neighborhoods, and societies in more Christian molds. Christians should not be fighting each other as to which is more important—love of God or love of fellow man. They should remember that the Bible tells us that the first command is to love God. They should also remember that the most effective way to bring about love of man is to multiply enormously the number of practicing Christians. Such multiplication must take place in every segment of society, in every nation-state. It would be naive to suppose that worldwide justice and righteousness can be instituted if only Europeans and Americans act justly and righteously. Righteousness in China is very largely determined by how Chinese treat each other. The same is true of every country.

There remains the question as to the right word for the Church's primary task. I hope that the word *mission* can be used solely for that activity of the Church which concerns reconciling men with God through belief in Jesus Christ, the Savior. English is a rich language. Many other words could be used for social justice and service—the Church's privilege, responsibility, or task, or God's command. When everything the Church should do—indeed, everything that God is doing in the world—is called the mission of God, discipling the nations disappears in a multitude of urgent local tasks.

What is at stake is not a mere word but rather how the treasure of Christian mission shall be used. The Church's investment in the evangelization of the world is not as great as it should be, but it is considerable—in annual givings, in headquarters buildings, in property across the seas, in training centers, in publishing houses, and in many other ways. This mission treasure has already been very greatly extended to cover many kinds of philanthropic missions. What we are now seeing is a drive to extend it still further to cover the promotion of friendly relations between labor and capital (disguised under the clever name *industrial evangelism*); the participation of Christians in revolutionary movements designed to achieve justice; the sharing in the war against fecundity; and many other good causes.

Let these all be done, but let them stand on their own merits and raise their own funds. Let us have done with this dishonest procedure that calls them all "mission," throws the mantle of "evangelism" over them, and uses funds gathered for propagating the gospel for these good enterprises which have very little to do with leading anyone into discipleship. Robbing the mission treasury should stop.

17

Fundraising and Discipling

Missionary societies are fundraising and missionary-sending organizations. But if they achieve only these essential ends, missionary societies can easily fail in carrying out the Great Commission. Most missionary societies should take the momentous decisions needed to guarantee that raising money and sending missionaries achieve their fundamental purpose.

Missionary societies are organizations and are subject to laws governing such. Parkinson's Law—that an organization tends to exist solely for its own continuation—applies to them as much as to any business organization. The organization is important. It must function. However, it should exist not for itself but for a specific end.

In business this means that the organization must make money. In science this means that the organization must either teach science or discover new scientific truths. In world evangelization this means that the organization must carry out God's command (Rom. 16:25–26) to make known the gospel to all peoples in such a way that *ethnos* after *ethnos* is led to faith and obedience.

Although most mission executives should agree that their societies do have and ought to have such a purpose, the unfortunate fact is that many a missionary society finds itself concerned chiefly if not solely with raising money, sending out missionaries, and keeping the machine running. Thus too often the missionary society does exist for

143

itself. The end is obscured while the organization flourishes. For example, it is beyond question that a chief function of a missionary society is to recruit missionaries and raise the money needed for their support, transportation, and work. If this is not done, nothing will happen. Yet it is also true that if only this is done, supremely well done, often nothing happens. It is not enough for the machine to function well as a machine. Smooth operation of a missionary society is not the end. The *effective* proclamation of the gospel to the ends of the earth and the reconciliation of multitudes to God in the Church of Jesus Christ are the biblical ends. It is not enough that the society sends out missionaries to proclaim the gospel. It must also know how effectively the gospel is being proclaimed and whether it could be proclaimed more effectively.

The missionary society is sensitive to its function as a fundraising and missionary-sending organization. It defends this function and uses new ideas in carrying it out. It is no accident that when missionary societies begin to use computers, they first use them to list and maintain contact with donors. No missionary society—to the best of my knowledge—uses computers to measure the disciplings it is already attempting and to discover how better to disciple those segments of society in which it is working. This is because missionary societies, as bureaus, are not nearly as sensitive to whether men and women are being reconciled or the peoples are being discipled.

For example, Cal Guy says:

> Just living makes considerable demands on the missionary's time. If the minutes spent in shopping, residence upkeep, maintenance of the auto, radio, and other western conveniences were added up, the total would in most cases be staggering. . . . A week spent in hearing missionaries plan their next year's work is illuminating. Budgets, salary scales, repairs, rents, and scholarships take hours. While the bulk of their planning ought to concern the spiritual thrust, most of it deals with matters material and mechanical.[1]

In private conversation Guy told me, "I have never known a missionary society to make guidance at this point a definite part of its program. The missionaries are out there. That is all the society cares. Clearing

---

1. Cal Guy, "Eliminating Underbrush in Church Growth and Christian Mission," in *Church Growth and Christian Mission*, ed. Donald A. McGavran (New York: Harper and Row, 1965), pp. 144, 146.

away the underbrush so the valuable timber trees can grow is not a part of the concern of the missionary society. It says, 'That is the business of the missionary. Whether he does it or not is of no concern to us. We assume he is doing it as well as can possibly be done.'"

A missionary of long experience once said sadly,

> I have been here for forty years. During a few of these years we have had good increase. In two notable years we baptized over five hundred believers; but in most years, the harvest of souls was much smaller and in many we had no baptism at all. I have never once received a letter from my missionary society either commending me during the years of harvest or comforting me during the years when we brought no sheaves to the Master's threshing floor. Once when the president of our society made a journey to this field, I took him out to the hills on muleback to see the twenty five little congregations God had raised up there during the time of my labors. In the book the president wrote about his world tour, the only comment he made on my station was to exclaim about what an adventurous horseman I was. If anyone wanted an exciting ride, he was advised to come and see me.

The president was a humane and kindly man but obviously more interested in creating the image of a missionary which he thought would appeal to the supporters of the society than he was in the twenty five congregations planted—the fundamental outcome of mission.

An experienced mission executive of the Baptist General Conference, Virgil Olson, says,

> Churches with strong unified budgets tend to cut down foreign mission. Foreign missions has to give in to the smallest and least item on the unified budget. The competition for the percentage on the unified budget becomes fierce in some denominational groups. Richard Hutcheson in his little book, *Wheel Within the Wheel*, shows that denominations with the unified budget lose out in missionary giving.

> Another concern in raising money for missions is that it is easy to permit promotion for money to dictate the philosophy of mission, rather than the other way around. If people will respond to this appeal, then the mission falls prey to the money resources. Consequently, it is not easy to raise money for church planting. It has no appeal to many of our churches.

It is not easy to resolve this conflict. While bureaus are set up to get things done, they must survive and continue. Thus survival becomes their chief end. Many bureaus, including missionary societies, find it difficult to hold the goal clearly in view, measure success and failure in terms of that goal, frankly agree that they have failed in some areas, and rectify procedures until they succeed.

Bureaus are conservative by nature. They dare not rock the boat. Too much is at stake and too many persons depend on the society being able, year after year, to raise one hundred thousand dollars or ten million dollars. They become prisoners of their system. They hesitate to undertake new activities, even those they are convinced will benefit the propagation of the gospel. This can be seen on many fronts.

Consider discipling of new, receptive peoples. The general secretary of a missionary society with an annual income of well over five million dollars said to me, "It would, of course, be desirable to move resources to meet these new opportunities, but it would take a dictator to do it and would run the risk of breaking up the missionary society." Many executives as well as many missionaries see opportunities which they feel unable to respond to because the welfare of the organization depends on carrying on existing work.

Take the vital subject of missionary training, both for candidates and career missionaries. There is general agreement that in order to achieve the goals of mission a much more intensive and extensive system of training is needed. In California, teachers in grade schools frequently are called in for a refresher course. Many of them go on to earn their masters degrees or doctoral degrees. The thirty-six thousand Protestant missionaries sent out from North America would profit greatly by a training program of this sort. If done cooperatively it would not be very expensive. Yet aside from candidate training, which some mission boards do well, almost all further training is left to a few seminaries and to those secular graduate schools of history, sociology, anthropology, or education near to which the missionary spends his furlough. Further training in effective mission, a discipline in its own right, is something the mission boards could to advantage do a great deal more of.

Take a common information pool. Some years ago I said to the Africa secretary of the Division of Foreign Missions in New York that Christian mission really ought to have a large-scale map of Africa on which every highly receptive tribe or population would be portrayed in scarlet, every mildly receptive tribe in pink, every friendly tribe in white, and hostile resistant tribes in green. This would help all missionary societies send resources to the most receptive populations. It would reinforce surging people movements. It would multiply sound churches. He agreed heartily that it would be very useful to have that information. But to date, in the Protestant world at least, there is no such map. This is no accident. The missionary society is a delicate fundraising and missionary-sending system. Anything beyond this it honestly feels is not its business and may rock the boat. That is, such work may interfere with what it perceives as its real job—getting missionaries out there and money in here.

The costly decisions that obedience to Christ requires are those which insist that, in addition to sending missionaries and raising money, the effectiveness of every missionary enterprise be carefully measured. Mission executives should be accurately informed on this point. They should also know how effectiveness has been achieved in other similar populations and come to well-based judgments as to how effectiveness would be increased in the populations for which their society is responsible.

The Christian and Missionary Alliance (C & MA) in 1978 made a momentous decision of this kind. It said in effect,

> Let us find out exactly the membership, rate of growth, receptivity of populations being evangelized for each of our mission fields. Let us then as a denomination and missionary society resolve before God to double our worldwide membership by 1987. From now on ministers and denominational leaders in America and missionaries and ministers overseas will work toward this challenging goal. We believe that it can be accomplished. With God's help it will be accomplished.

This resolution was implemented under the dynamic leadership of E. L. King, president of the General Council of C&MA. In late 1983 the Reverend David Moore, vice president of overseas ministries, wrote that the overseas churches are right on target.

Not all missionary societies will be able to achieve such a dramatic goal, but all of them can and many of them will find out where the churches they are establishing are and are not growing and what needs to be done in order to make them effective instruments of God's grace. Whether they set a decadal growth rate of 100 percent or 20 percent as their goal will depend on circumstances. If they do this, they will not be doing just good mission work; they will be carrying out God's command.

In short, the momentous decisions required to make missionary societies more effective will be those which direct attention to the degree to which existing efforts are in fact leading people after people to faith and obedience.

Part 4

Momentous
Strategic Decisions

18

The Entrepreneur
in Modern Missions

Dictionaries define an entrepreneur as one who organizes, operates, and assumes risk for a business venture. The term indicates that combination of mind, character, and spirit which is the lifeblood of organizations of all dimensions.

William H. Donaldson, Dean of the Yale School of Organization and Management, says,

> Entrepreneurship involves an ability to think abstractly about the *fundamental purpose of an organization*, and at the same time, a capacity to *develop strategies and implement tactics* necessary to achieve that purpose. . . . Entrepreneurship requires a blending of individual participation . . . with the creating of a management structure whose ultimate flexibility and sensitivity to human needs assures its future durability.[1]

The Church is an organization. So is the missionary society. Both, therefore, have fundamental purposes. Both develop strategies and tactics necessary to achieve those purposes.

1. *Yale Alumni Magazine*, April 1978. Italics added.

151

A Fundamental Purpose of the Church

One of the fundamental purposes of the Church is to spread the faith, to preach the gospel, and to persuade the peoples of earth to follow Christ, who is the Light of the nations. The Church which is sealed off, turned in on itself, and not interested in bringing the good news of salvation to all men is a religious club. It is not the Church of Jesus Christ. The missionary society also lives to proclaim Christ and persuade men to become His disciples and responsible members of His Church. An organization which does not pursue this purpose may be an instrument for social engineering or an inter-racial harmonizer, but it is not a missionary society. The entre-preneur identifies the fundamental purpose and then "develop[s] strategies and implement[s] tactics" necessary to achieve that pur-pose.

Executives of missionary societies, professors of missions, and missionaries are what business management calls entrepreneurs. Using the word helps us think about the fundamental purpose of missions and about strategies and tactics which further it. My thesis is that constantly "think[ing] abstractly about the fundamental pur-pose" of missions and constantly "develop[ing] strategies and imple-ment[ing] tactics necessary to achieve that purpose" are normal missionary activities. Using these contemporary business terms helps us think clearly about our task.

While the fundamental purpose remains the same year after year and century after century, strategies change. Tactics change still more. Every new shift of the wind requires a new tactic. To illustrate this, I record five strategies I developed to meet the changing situations in missions during the last quarter century. Readers might well contem-plate what changes in strategy they themselves developed and imple-mented as they held to their fundamental purpose in the varying circumstances of the past two decades. Changes in strategy and tactics must be made frequently.

1. In the early fifties it became clear to me that the mission-station approach, also called the gathered-colony approach, which all around the world was necessary to the beginning stages of the propagation of the gospel, in later stages actually thwarted the main purpose of the Church and of Christian mission. I devoted years to developing

strategies and implementing tactics which would surmount this
difficulty and get church and mission back to achieving their main
purpose.

2. In the later fifties, I discerned that lack of interest in the actual
discipling of the nations was defeating the fundamental purpose of
both church and mission. That lack of interest sometimes arose from
organizational causes, sometimes from theological. Sometimes it
arose from excess zeal in perfecting those segments of humanity
which had been discipled. It closed its eyes to the enormous numbers
who had no way of hearing the good news.

In the late fifties, therefore, my overriding concern was to direct
attention to this deflection and to devise strategies and tactics that
would return church and mission to emphasizing the fundamental
purpose.

3. In the early sixties, holding steadily before me the fundamental
purpose of church and mission to bring the *ethnē* to faith and
obedience (Rom. 16:25–26), I saw that lack of anthropological
knowledge on the part of missionaries and sociological knowledge on
the part of ministers often meant that the main goal of church and
mission was only partially reached, if indeed it was reached at all. I
consequently developed strategies which drew heavily on the social
sciences. I called to my faculty anthropologists and loaded the
curriculum with courses in anthropology, sociology, communication
science, and the like.

4. In the late sixties and the seventies, I suddenly realized that the
theology of mission developed by the conciliar wing of the Church was
quietly scuttling discipling of the nations. Until February 1968 this was
not clear to me; but when I saw the preparatory papers for the Fourth
Assembly of the World Council of Churches, the disturbing incidents I
had noticed for several years fell into place. The "new mission" which
had been developed stood out as plain as a pikestaff. What strategy is
needed, I asked myself, to bring mission back to the classical-biblical
foundation? The answer was: Point out in great detail the way in
which "new mission," while it uses the old sacred words, means
something totally different. Point out to both evangelical and conciliar
forces that totally new theology and theory of what is called mission
have been developed and are being actively advocated. That was the
strategy the entrepreneur had to develop. He implemented tactics to
gain that end.

5. In the eighties I see the fundamental purpose of the Church and the Christian mission being denied in a new direction. World evangelization is being badly damaged by the following powerful factor. The older, stronger Churches, motivated by a commendable desire to treat the younger, weaker Churches with respect, have surrendered all initiative in evangelism to them. Arguments like the following support this drastic move: "The leaders of the overseas Churches, knowing the language and the customs of the people intuitively, can evangelize more effectively than missionaries from outside the country. Missionaries are expensive. For what one missionary costs, five national evangelists can be supported. It is often difficult and sometimes impossible to get missionaries into a country. When missionaries evangelize, the nationals sit on their hands and do nothing. For missionaries to evangelize gives the impression that Christianity is a foreign religion. If new congregations start with help from foreigners, they lack the rugged self-direction which all churches ought to have." Each of these arguments, and others which could be mentioned, can easily be answered, but they are nevertheless tendered and to a degree, at least, believed.

The net outcome is that huge populations in many lands are left without witness. Evangelization seldom goes on outside the immediate neighborhood of existing churches. The younger denominations do not carry on cross-cultural evangelism in any but the smallest measure. Nor do they invite missionary societies of other countries to come in and do the evangelization needed.

A novel and erroneous doctrine has been developed and is widely influential—namely, that the whole land "belongs" to one of the denominations in that land, and no missionary society from another land should send in missionaries unless specifically asked to do so by its sister denomination. For example, in Freetown, Sierra Leone, among the Creole population, which speaks English, the Anglican Church is strong. The tribal populations east of Freetown are solidly pagan, in the process of becoming Muslim. But no Anglican missionary society dreams of sending missionaries to these tribes— which are rather receptive. Unless the Creole Church specifically asks them to send missionaries, Anglicans in Britain, Canada, and the United States will send none. Initiative has been surrendered to the national Church. Often after a missionary society has ceased to send missionaries, they will not be sent even if the younger Church asks for them. The older Church has lost the ability to send missionaries. It has so long taken shelter behind the comfortable doctrine that the younger Church—wonderful people, you know—will do the job, that it finds it extraordinarily difficult to recruit, support, send, and administer a mission in another land. Furthermore, were missionaries to be sent to Sierra Leone, they would likely be used in teaching school or otherwise enriching the life of the Creole Christians. The Creole Churches in Freetown or its neighborhood would not send them to carry on pioneer missions among the Mende, Kissi, or other tribesmen of that land.

The fault is often that of the mission, not the younger Church. A board sends missionaries to work with the Church. The mission finds that it can locate missionaries chiefly in the urban centers which have electricity, running water, interior plumbing, and a good postal service. The Church would send the missionaries out to the hinterland but cannot do so. In desperation, the fatuous suggestion of a moratorium on missionaries is voiced. Moratorium, when three billion have yet to believe! Missionaries sent to the Creole Church in Sierra Leone might in very truth, with the best of intentions on both sides, stay in or near Freetown and keep the Church from exerting itself. They might even dominate it. Under these circumstances the missionary society concerned not only should launch a major new program of evangelism and avoid burdening the young Church with administering it, but also should educate its missionaries in frontier missions and send to the field chiefly those whom God calls to evangelize the unreached.

Today in many instances when missionaries are sent, elaborate documents are drawn up—almost as detailed as those which govern the stationing of foreign troops on the soil of a sister nation. The relationships of the missionaries to the Church, whose orders they must obey, what meetings they can convene, and the like, are all laid down in writing. Often the missionary is frustrated because he is so hemmed in by regulations. Often the national feels that if the missionary were not there, the work would go better. The attention is taken off the job to be done, the gospel to be proclaimed, new churches to be multiplied, and responsive peoples to be identified and evangelized. Instead it is focused on the relationships of the missionary to the existing congregations and denominational structures.

The Missionary Society as Entrepreneur

Let us dream. Suppose the Church Missionary Society, whose headquarters are in London, were to say to the Anglican Church in Sierra Leone,

> Dear friends, we intend to send a force of twenty missionaries to occupy a territory of two thousand square miles one hundred miles southeast of Freetown, and want your blessing on the enterprise. It will cost you nothing. We shall employ some of your members in various capacities, but will not burden you with the administration of the enterprise. That will rest solely on the mission. The mission will operate under the genial supervision of the Sierra Leonian bishop in Freetown, but will take very little of his time. We hope to have a Christian community of fifty thousand from that tribe within twenty years. When it becomes strong and self-supporting, it will, of course, form part of the Anglican Church in Sierra Leone—linguistically and ethnically different from you and yet part of your great brotherhood.

Were any such proposal to be made at present, it would be hooted down.[2] Under the poisonous doctrine that all of Sierra Leone "belongs" to the Creole Church, even when it does no evangelization outside its own neighborhood, the Church Missionary Society does not dare exercise any evangelistic initiative. Unless the national Church acts, there will be little spreading of the Good News. Even if God were to direct the Missionary Society to send missionaries, this poisonous doctrine would not permit God's command to be heard. Mind you, the young Church concerned can keep out only its friends. It cannot keep out Roman Catholics, Pentecostals, Seventh-Day Adventists, or Muslims. A Baptist church cannot keep out determined Lutherans, but it can keep out fellow Baptists.

I need not labor the point. Surrender of initiative in evangelism to national denominations—done with the best of motives on both sides, of course—has led and is leading to major failure in achieving the fundamental purpose of both church and mission. The disease afflicts

---

2. The 189th General Assembly of the United Presbyterian Church in the U.S.A. (1977) affirms the Program Agency guideline that the "primary responsibility for sharing the good news in each and every country lies with the indigenous church." *Minutes of the General Assembly of the United Presbyterian Church of the United States of America*, 7th series, vol. 11 (New York: Office of the General Assembly, 1977), p. 548.

many denominations. Camouflaged as it is under the guise of exercising the respect due to sovereign nations and treating our overseas brothers with scrupulous fairness, surrender of evangelistic initiative quietly sabotages the basic ends of Christian mission.

Consequently, I have recently bent my energies to developing strategies and implementing tactics to enable both missions and churches to devote themselves to the supreme and controlling purpose of the Christian mission to the world. It is clear that the honor and respect due to churches in other lands ought to be preserved. This will best be done by evangelizing beyond them, if possible with their blessing, but without burdening them with administering such efforts. The missions (from Japan, Korea, the Philippines, India, England, Germany, Kenya, and Brazil, to mention only a few lands which are now sending their own nationals abroad as missionaries) ought to be mobile, lean, and effective. They ought to call recruits to lifetime service and give them every incentive for learning the language and culture of the peoples being evangelized. Each mission would appoint one of its number to effect liaison with its sister Church in that land. The mission would also form the clusters of new congregations into a denomination of like precious faith and polity. I believe such strategy and tactics would be cordially welcomed by young Churches everywhere. These new missions would absorb missionaries at present working—perhaps longer than they should— with old, established denominations. Occasionally when the younger Church really needs missionary assistance, negotiations could be undertaken to invite some missionary or missionaries back into a ministry in an already functioning denomination. Were the task sufficiently urgent, missionary society and Church administrators would readily work out the details.

Only one real obstacle remains. Sending Churches (whether in Tanzania, Norway, Indonesia, Taiwan, Chile, Mexico, California, or Canada) might spend most of their resources on the new missions and have little left to assist the already established congregations and clusters of congregations. Overseas Churches might argue that the missionary society has only so much money and this new strategy will deprive them of useful subsidies to their boarding schools, hospitals, agricultural demonstration centers, and seminaries. What shall we say to this objection?

First, although this is obviously possible, it is not likely. The missionary societies and sending denominations are the best friends the younger Churches have. They are their founding fathers. They will certainly feel that the new Churches should do all they can—but so will all responsible leaders of the new Churches.

Second, the establishment of new clusters of congregations in the land gives the denominations there the best possible help. It increases their weight in the national scene. It brings to them a rich variety of cultural inheritances. It keeps already established denominations from becoming ingrown and ghettoized. By focusing attention on the continuing task of world evangelization, it helps young Churches to be fully church and to share in the essential work of Christ.

Third, nothing will stimulate young Churches more than the vivid possibility of their missionary assistants moving on fifty or five hundred miles to unreached peoples. Moving on helps the Church avoid introversion and helps it grow in love and service, knowledge and power, and obedience to the Savior who commands us all, "Go, disciple the nations."

Let me now confess that I have used the word *entrepreneur* as a device to center attention on the fundamental purpose of church and mission and on the necessity of devising strategies and tactics that will seize the opportunities and surmount the obstacles before the Church. I am confident many will join me in seeking to be better stewards of the grace of God. Let us be more obedient to God's command to make Christ known, believed, and loved in all quarters of the globe.

Doing this will require carefully researched appraisals of the opportunities of the contemporary world and costly moves to transfer resources out of the less obedient and effective of our programs, strategies, and tactics into those which carry out better Christ's fundamental purpose to seek and save the lost and return wandering sons and daughters to their Father's house.

19

Missions in France?

The most momentous decisions of the day can often be seen best in the concrete. Rather than asking, "Should we carry on missions to peer nations today?" I ask, "What about Christian missions to France?"

Americans may well say, "France is a peer nation. The United States owes much to France. Had it not been for French assistance and sympathy, an independent America might never have been born. Culturally, artistically, and in the realm of letters and science, our nation is deeply indebted to our sister republic. Indeed, since John Calvin was a great Frenchman, all Protestant denominations are under obligation to France." Furthermore, France has a vast Christian heritage. France today, according to David B. Barrett, sends out twenty-three thousand missionaries to the non-Christian world. France, like all other European countries, regards itself as a Christian country. Its cathedrals are famous. Its theologians write books that are read in many countries. Why then send missionaries to France or any other "Christian" country? Should missionary societies regard France as a mission field, seek out receptive segments of French society, and disciple them? As we answer those questions, we can make the momentous decisions regarding other peer nations—other "Christian" countries.

Mission to Peer Nations

Today more and more mission must be carried out in peer nations. The day when ruler nations carried out mission in subject lands is gone. With it should disappear the common opinion that mission proceeds from "have" to "have-not" lands and consists essentially in "doing something for those poor people." One has but to observe that Christian mission in the New Testament proceeded from the "have-nots" to the "haves," from the provinces to Rome, from Galilee to Athens, and from the poor to the wealthy, to see that the common opinion is not valid. Mission—purposeful evangelization—must not be done exclusively in developing nations. It intends to lead men to accept Jesus Christ, the Son of God, the Savior of the world. Men and women of nations at a high level of economic, educational, and technological development need Christ just as much as illiterate, landless laborers in developing nations. Both must be evangelized.

Subject nations have all but vanished. Poor nations have not, but may yet do so. In any case, since mission will be carried out from many sending lands—from India as well as America, Congo as well as Canada, and Brazil as well as Germany—it is time that Christians realize that mission goes to peer nations quite as readily as to backward nations. On occasion, it properly goes to peoples who have greater possessions, military might, educational insight, and cultural advance than the sending church.

I am not talking in the loose current sense, wherein mission is everything God might wish churches or Christians to do. I am using the term *mission* in the classic sense—namely, that it consists of all those words and deeds which intend to proclaim Jesus Christ as divine and only Savior and to persuade men to become His disciples and responsible members of His Church. What about this kind of mission in France?

Some Christian leaders of other lands will at once object that, since France is a Christian country, mission should be directed not to her but to non-Christian lands where the great majority has neither heard the name nor had the opportunity to believe on the Savior. Some French Christians will at once say that for the United States to send missionaries to France with the purpose of winning its citizens to the divine life is both impertinent and unnecessary. Presumably most babies born in France have been baptized in the name of the Father, Son, and Holy Spirit. They have grown up considering themselves in some vague way as Christians. "After all," they say, "we are French-men. And all Frenchmen are, of course, Christians." Why then send missionaries to them? Were they to be converted to some ardent branch of the Church, would not this constitute "sheep stealing"? Is not missionary activity of this sort exactly the kind of labor in which Christians should *not* engage? In this cold, hungry, and oppressed world should not Christians be working with men of other lands to achieve a more just, more peaceful, and better-clothed world, rather than selfishly trying to win them into their own ecclesiastical organizations?

Questions like these put the issue sharply. As we consider it, we shall be thinking about our brothers and sisters in France, our equals and our betters. What about proclaiming Jesus Christ to them and persuading them to become His responsible followers?

The essential question is, Do all Frenchmen accept Jesus Christ as their personal Lord and Savior? That they live in a "Christian country" is immaterial. That they were born of parents who with or without good reason counted themselves Christian is inconsequential. That they were baptized as infants has no bearing on the issue at all, unless that early baptism is validated by a current obedient relationship to the Head. A view of baptism which makes it akin to branding calves which thereafter belong to a rancher is totally unbiblical. Baptism does not signify, "This man belongs to my Church. If you bring him to ardent faith in Christ and add him to your Church, you are stealing my property."

If in France men and women can be found who do not know the Savior, then no matter what religion they formally profess, they are proper subjects of mission. And should large numbers of French citizens openly proclaim that they are adherents of no religion, that they are agnostics, atheists, Marxists, positivists, or secularists, Christian mission among them is not only defensible but also commanded by God. He does not wish that any should perish. He wishes all to come to active intentional discipleship.

Countering Objections to Mission in Peer Nations

The question remains, Should such mission be carried out by the powerful French denominations (Lutheran, Reformed, Roman Catholic) or by denominations from across the seas—from Africa, Japan, or America? Two considerations should be borne in mind.

Theological Issues

From the theological point of view, none can object to Christians anywhere sending to non-Christians anywhere Christ-proclaiming ambassadors who intend to convert non-Christians. The world has grown too small and travel too rapid and easy to suggest that it would be impertinent for Jamaicans to proclaim Christ in California with the intent of winning secular citizens of this state to a joyful redemptive relationship to Jesus Christ in a denomination which called Jamaica home. When Hindu swamis make disciples in California, what Christian could possibly object to the spread of a Jamaica-based branch of the Christian Church? Indeed, just such churches are spreading. For example, in California, the True Jesus Churches of Taiwan are multiplying to the great benefit of those who find Christ in them. If a Baptist denomination based in Chicago spreads it branches abroad in La Belle France, there will be rejoicing in heaven. Theologically there can be no objection.

Pragmatically, however, legitimate objection must be raised. Should the Methodist Church in the French-speaking Ivory Coast send missionaries to France and maintain them there for decades at a cost which prevents it from discipling the responsive tribes of its own land? We are here in the realm of the prudential and expedient, and no one can lay down a general rule. It might be that missionaries from Ivory Coast would find themselves accepted and their support assumed by their converts in France. The missionaries might, indeed, send back money for the saints in some Ivory Coast "Jerusalem" with the result that the discipling of the pagan tribes there was advantaged. All one can say is that since there is no theological objection, the questions of expediency will in each case have to be answered in the light of what is financially, socially, and politically profitable.

"Ah, but," someone is certain to exclaim, "you have too rapidly passed by a real theological objection. Any such missionizing assists the multiplication of divisive sects in the Church. It actually promotes schism, and schism is sin." This objection deserves careful reply. The unity of the Church is truly precious. It should be a goal of our prayers and labors. Yet having said this, let us note first that the Church is of necessity split into thousands of branch Churches which never see each other and never have anything to do with each other. Differences of language, location, income, education, political opinion, and historical association make different branches of each denomination substantially strangers to one another. A Roman Catholic, James O. McGovern, asks, "Is there 'one' Church or rather is there not one faith which makes all Churches 'one'?"[1] Does a new, ardently Christian Church in France, organizationally separate from Reformed, Lutheran, and Roman Catholic Churches, really "split" the Body of Christ? Can any reasonable man maintain this? Is such a "new" Church not glorifying God through adding more room to the sheepfold? Since the Lord is one, is not the Body one?

Second, is it really better to leave nominal, cold, and lapsed Christians "in their sins" and in their ancestral church than to win them as genuine Christians into some organizationally separate branch of the Church? Can anyone imagine that it would be more pleasing to God? True, if each existing Church would be renewed and sally forth with zeal to reclaim its own lost, it could do so with the least expenditure of effort. Roman Catholics in France could win to ardent discipleship the thirty million nominal Catholics there much more economically than could Canadian Presbyterian missionaries. But what if they do not? What if they will not? Is there any better way to motivate them than for the Presbyterians, Pentecostals, and Anglicans from Canada to win five million Frenchmen into Presbyterian, Pentecostal, and Anglican churches?

Let me now confess. I have been writing not merely about France. I have been writing about missions to peer countries, using France as an illustration and arguing that if mission to France were valid, it would be valid to all lands. By the way, if anyone finds this illustration about France uncomfortable, let him start justifying mission to Japan. He will discover that the arguments he uses to justify mission to an advanced and educated nation such as Japan (now having the fourth highest standard of living in the world) will apply equally well to France. Both have millions of men and women, boys and girls who do not know Jesus Christ. That is the basic fact which justifies and demands mission.

The Influence of Secularism

Also to be considered is that a vast tide of Secularism has swept over Europe and North America. In "Christian" countries it is common for only a small percent of the population to attend church. In a city of thirty thousand in the United States a pastor told me that

---

1. James O. McGovern, *The Church in the Churches* (Washington, D.C.: Corpus, 1968), p. 172.

six out of seven of the people living there never attend church. In Scandinavia one hears that only 5 percent of the population attend church. A German pastor recently told me that four thousand souls live in his parish. Of these, one hundred attend church; he had contact with three hundred more, and with thirty-six hundred he had no contact at all.

If the tide of Secularism is to be rolled back, tremendous new and effective evangelism must be carried on. One hopes much of this will be carried on by the Christians of that particular nation, but if Christians from other nations come there to evangelize, who can object?

It would be arrogant for Christians to say to developing nations, "If your sons and daughters do not know Christ, we shall in the name of religious liberty claim the right to send missionaries to you; but if our sons and daughters do not know Him, you cannot send missionaries to us." The Churches of Europe and America cannot maintain that while nominal (and practicing) Muslims, animists, Hindus, Jews, and Buddhists should be evangelized, nominal Christians must not be.

The Issue of Religious Liberty

The doctrine of religious liberty also bears upon the issue. Religious liberty—each person worshiping and propagating his religion as he pleases—is an inalienable human right. Persuasion and counter-persuasion are the stuff life is made of. All scientific advance is based on the premise that in an open market truth will prevail. Christian missionaries have played an important part in securing this right for all men. In claiming it for themselves, often risking their lives to do so, they won it for others.

Now, since France would be the first to maintain that Muslims, Buddhists, Marxists, and other religionists have a right to practice and propagate their faith in France, she has no recourse but to extend the same right to any Christian denomination. Nor need any Church or missionary society evangelizing France do so with an uneasy conscience. The more churches it plants there, providing only that they are reasonably biblical and vital, the better it is for France.

Evangelizing Peer Nations Encourages Christian Nurture

The tendency today for some missiologists to think of evangelism and church planting in derogatory terms, as if it were an imperialistic and unfriendly raid on the territory of a neighbor nation, is fanciful. The assumption that intercourse among the great religions is best promoted not by church planting missions but by quiet dialogue and genial reconception of each religion (by its own adherents, of course) in the light of other religions, is manufactured in the ivory towers of academia. Nothing promotes intercourse between two religions more effectively than the establishment of churches of each in the territory of the other. Then dialogue is carried on not by intellectuals on infrequent occasions in the rarified atmosphere of interfaith meetings but by robust adherents of each religion every hour of every day in the myriad contacts of the marketplace and factory, political campaign and corporation management.

Evangelism is the friendliest possible activity. If to become a Christian, know Christ as Lord and Savior, have one's sins forgiven, and be empowered to act lovingly in this unlovely world is the pearl of great price, what greater boon can Christians confer on their neighbors than to lead them to these pearls? We should not hesitate to extend the principle to non-Christians. If Muslims hold that to believe on Allah and Mohammed is the ultimate good, they are unfriendly if they do not do their best to share this good with Christian lands. If Marxists really believe that the dictatorship of the proletariat is the way to utopia, they would be unfriendly if they did not send missionaries to spread their doctrine. Whether they will be able to spread it, of course, will depend on its truth and their own exertions. And as they are free to proclaim it, I remain free to disbelieve it. The principle remains, however—sending missionaries to peer countries to carry the best we know is a legitimate and friendly activity.

The best defense each religion has against the encroachments of other religions (I am using provocative terminology) is not to stigmatize missionizing as illegitimate and to bar it from the land but to improve itself to the place where its adherents cannot be persuaded. Hungry sheep are the ones impelled toward offers of food. Perhaps we should say that sheep stealing is a myth. Well-fed sheep cannot be stolen. Only those running wild, hungry, and neglected can be led to other folds—and leading them there is commendable, not reprehensible.

In the era now opening out before the religions of the world, extensive conversion missions will become common and will encourage all religions to improve their own shepherding. Religions which provide inadequate care will and should lose their adherents. Is this true? It would mean, for example, that if some Church now powerful in France (Lutheran, Reformed, or Roman) neglected its own, failed to instruct them in the Christian faith, permitted the divine fire to burn low within them, and allowed them to drift to nominalism, unbelief, Marxism, and other faiths, it would wither and if not revived would die. The same principle will operate in all lands. For example, if animism does not feed its millions, they will go elsewhere.

The old national, linguistic, and folk barriers, which kept Christians of a given variety loyal to a Church which systematically starved them, are disappearing. "Feed them or lose them" is rapidly coming to be an operative principle all over the world.

Will this principle apply equally to Christian and non-Christian religions? Christians believe that when a person has once received eternal life in Jesus Christ, has once believed on Him and accepted His sacrifice on Calvary for himself, he is then fed. Some denominations believe that, if this transaction has really taken place, the Christian cannot lose his salvation—that is, in this context he cannot be led astray to some pseudosavior. When members of such denominations are led astray (and they are), it is held that they were never truly saved in the first place. Be that as it may, everyone would agree that enormous numbers of Christians, accepted as members of even the strictest Churches, are living out of touch with their Head. Unless these are brought back into touch, whatever the theological explanation of the process may be, they are likely to be lost. Feed them or lose them! Because Christians believe that other religions cannot feed them, that truly "no man comes to the Father but by Jesus Christ," they will argue that the ill-fed Christian will gain more by staying a Christian than he will by going elsewhere. Indeed by going elsewhere he will starve to death, for only Christ is the living bread. Nevertheless, although the real Christian believes this, the nominal Christian doubts it. He can be recruited by false and inadequate religions, and can "labor for that which is not bread."

Despite the fact that the Church which loses members seldom admits that the Church which gains them can feed them better, men move according to how hungry *they* feel, not according to whether the doctrines of their Church teach that they should not be hungry.

Should all Churches, therefore, cease evangelism and begin most carefully to feed their members? By no means. Evangelism is one of the best ways in which to feed and nurture Christians. Christian nurture is not a static thing. The metaphor *food* must not be pressed too hard. Christian nurture involves of necessity the process of communicating one's faith. If it is not vital enough to be communicated, if the desire is not there to tell others about Jesus, the person is undernourished. If a man does not habitually work and pray that all men everywhere come to know, love, and obey the Savior, he is neglected. He is out of touch with his Head. He is out of communion with the Savior of men. He has no life in him. He is open to the wiles of the devil.

In the days which lie ahead the Churches need to create a theology which is at once thoroughly Christian and thoroughly geared to the new day when sending "converting missions" to peer nations will become common practice. The theological and ecclesiological presuppositions which state churches created in Europe and which Protestantism created in North America simply do not fit this pluralistic society. It is unthinkable that Christians will meet this new day by saying, "Since we live in a day when many religions exist side by side in perfect freedom, therefore all proclamation of Christ and all attempt to persuade men to become His baptized followers and members of His Church should cease." That is neither theologically nor sociologically sound; that is withdrawal from reality. Christians cannot take that route.

Neither the freedom of practice and propagation of what appears highest and truest, nor the conviction that there *is* a highest and a truest, may be surrendered. The new theology we need combines both emphases. It manufactures a new synthesis which remains biblically Christian in a pluralistic world.

20

Literature, Radio, and Principles of Growth

Literature is an important arm of Christian mission. Tracts, pamphlets, Gospels, books, stories, and addresses are written in hundreds of different languages, printed and sold, or given away. Literature reaches far beyond the actual presence of missionaries and national leaders. It is read in homes whose threshold is never crossed by any Christian. Literature is a most important tool of world evangelization.

This is also true of Christian radio. Much of what I say about Christian literature can be applied to Christian radio. So here and there throughout this chapter I shall speak about radio as well as literature.

We must therefore make sure that these tools are produced and distributed in accordance with the fundamental purpose which animates and controls all Christian mission. It is quite possible to produce literature which simply translates what has proved effective in Europe or America. It is equally possible to produce literature which, while thoroughly indigenous, does not emphasize the essential goal of all mission.

In order to make sure that Christian literature and radio are effective evangelism, let me lay before you three basic principles of church growth and set forth one or two applications for each. I shall be illustrating the kind of thinking we need to do and indicating something of the length and breadth of the area where culture, communication, and God's passion for the redemption of men intersect. I shall not exhaust these principles. Much more could be said and, indeed, should be said about each. Please accept what I say as a brief example of the treatment needed, a brief glimpse through an open window at an area of enormous importance for the creation and use of literature and radio.

I am dealing with one dimension only of the problem of Christian literature. I am not asking how Christian literature can be made self-supporting, what vocabulary and format will ensure wide reading of the material, what thought forms will present the truths of the Christian religion so that men will best understand them. If literature is to be used, these questions must be correctly answered. But I am probing a different dimension. We all realize that it is possible to have self-supporting Christian literature, the vocabulary and format of which assure wide reading, and which present Christianity in a way that men understand it—and yet get very little acceptance of Christ and very little growth of the Church! I am asking what we must do (beyond getting literature understandable, widely read, and self-supporting) to encourage acceptance of Christ, baptism of believers, and multiplication of ongoing congregations.

Promoting Growth and Discipling

The first basic principle of church growth is this: Church growth must be clearly intended, believing that it is a chief and irreplaceable goal of Christian mission. We must take the Great Commission seriously. One large missionary society phrased this basic principle as follows and observed it as its dominant purpose for more than fifty years: "The supreme and compelling purpose of the Christian mission to the world is to proclaim Jesus Christ as Lord and only Savior and to persuade men to become His disciples and responsible members of His Church." That is the long-range goal of Christian literature.

In literature published overseas by missions it is particularly important to hold firmly to the "supreme and compelling purpose of Christian mission." Often missionaries work in a resistant field. There at the beginning "becoming a Christian" seems to the people of the land an unknown and fearsome thing to do. A long period of little or no church growth is common. During this period, which may last for decades, we are tempted to forget the purpose and to do good work of some kind. In the midst of enormous human need there are always many good deeds waiting to be done. So we write tracts about flies, malaria, good citizenship, or even the gospel—whether anyone becomes Christian or not.

This temptation should be firmly resisted. Every piece of literature which has a discipling rather than a perfecting purpose should be conceived, written, printed, distributed, and prayed for with the supreme and controlling purpose of the mission in mind. Let me give you an example from the field of Bible distribution.

In the early seventies a certain organization planned to fly ten million copies of the Gospel of John into the People's Republic of China. These were to be wrapped in plastic bags and dropped in rice paddies. The anticipation was that when they were found the Gospels would be secreted and quietly distributed from person to person. Some copies, of course, would be surrendered to the authorities and burned.

Hearing of this, a friend wrote to this organization to ask that each of the Gospels of John include this on the last page:

> Form an association of your close and trusted friends to study this book. Then give your minds and wills and lives to Jesus Christ who walks the earth today and is God at work. Study His Word. Pray to Him. Obey all His commands made known to you in this book and by His speaking to your own hearts. Do this openly if you can; secretly if you cannot. All who truly commit their lives to the Lord Jesus and live as His disciples—studying, praying, obeying—will be saved, will receive power, will be indwelt by the Holy Spirit. Associations may be of any size, from two persons to two hundred. They meet by day, by night, in homes, in caves, in the fields, and in village squares to worship God according to His revelation in this book. They learn His will for them, and live as sons of God.

The organization replied:

> Our board of operation has prayed about your letter. Although our original plans were to have no markings, identifications, names, dates, places, or additions other than the Gospel of John, we have felt led of the Lord to add a page giving a translation of your paragraph without

name or comments. Your suggestion is beautiful and a blessing to our
hearts.

Without the last page the distribution of the Gospels tended heavily
in the direction of seed sowing as an end. With that last page,
emphasis shifted to bringing the people of China to faith and
obedience (Rom. 16:25–26).

Much Christian literature should be distributed with the hope and
prayer that readers, by simply reading the pamphlet or book, will
become followers of the Lord Jesus Christ. They will gather their
family members, intimates, and trusted neighbors into a house
church. This might meet openly. It might meet in extreme secrecy. It
might identify with some existing congregation or denomination. It
might remain entirely separate. In many places men and women do
not become Christians because, although they love the Lord, they do
not wish to unite and worship with the existing church. Perhaps their
language is different. Their culture is different. Their standard of
living is different. Or they feel that the existing church is a foreign
institution from which they should remain entirely separate. An
invitation to form home Bible-study groups, Christian cells, house
churches, or other such organizations might well be a regular part of
much Christian literature. This is particularly true in resistant populations where "to become a Christian" means to join an existing
congregation and is scorned as joining the enemy.

To take another example, here is a Bible correspondence course. Its
true aim is *not* merely to study a Gospel but rather so to study it that
the students believe in Jesus Christ, repent of their sins, are baptized,
and are added to the Church—either to an existing congregation or to
an entirely new one in some unreached people. This aim, if clear in
the mind of the person who prepares the course, will be implemented
in suitable ways in the directions for study and the examinations.

Tracts, which are tools of enormous power, should never be "just
tracts." They should always be high-conversion-potential (HCP)
tracts. In 1956 I did a survey of church growth for the United Church
of Christ in the Philippines. I concluded:

The literature we describe is aimed at producing church growth. It has
HCP. We are not speaking of literature on morality, rural reconstruc-
tion, literacy, public health, stewardship, young peoples conferences,
and church organization—necessary as all these good things are. We

are speaking of tracts which get on with the central continuing task of
the world mission—discipling the nations and multiplying conversions
and churches.[1]

The first basic principle is that church growth must be clearly
intended, since we believe it to be God's will. Church growth is rooted
in theology. Policies concerning Christian literature must be theologically right. This, of course, means that the literature must be sound as
to the basic doctrines of the Christian religion. But it must also be
sound as to God's salvational purpose. It must be filled with Christ's
passion that men be reconciled to God through Christ in His Church.
This biblical position must inform and direct policies which have to
do with goals, priorities, and emphases in all Christian literature.

Communicating the Gospel to Specific Groups

The second basic principle is that major church growth ordinarily
takes place in receptive units of the population. Church growth is
rooted not only in theology, but also in sociology. Communicating
Christ never takes place in a vacuum. It always occurs among men;
men exist in societies. They do not exist as separate units like stones in
a pile but rather in societies, like knots in a tennis net, all linked
together with other members of their particular segment of society.
Men exist as classes, tribes, castes, clans, families, and language
groups.

In Chicago there are Puerto Ricans, Irish Catholics, German
Catholics, blacks, recent migrants from Appalachia, and numerous
other blocks of humanity. Mankind exists as a mosaic made up of
hundreds of separate pieces, hundreds of separate societies.

Incidentally, the concept *mankind* is a myth. There is no "mankind"; all we can see are thousands of pieces of the human mosaic.
The great theologian Friedrich Schleiermacher, making this same
point, took his students to a restaurant. "Waiter," he said, "bring me
some fruit." The waiter hurriedly brought him a tray full of apples,
pears, and grapes. Schleiermacher angrily dashed it to the ground.
"Waiter!" he roared, "I told you to bring me some *fruit*. All you bring
me are apples, pears, and grapes." Then he turned to his amazed
students. "You see," he continued, "in all the world there is no fruit.

1. Donald A. McGavran, *Multiplying Churches in the Philippines* (Manila: United Church of
Christ in the Philippines, 1958), pp. 102–3.

All we see are specific fruits. All generalizations are nonexistent. Only the specific truly exists." All we see are the thousands of different pieces of the mosaic of mankind.

The mosaic is enormously more complex abroad. In the United States almost everyone speaks English, reads the same newspapers, listens to the same broadcasts, and drives the same kind of cars. But abroad, the different pieces of the mosaic commonly speak radically different languages and live in radically different places. In Indonesia, for example, are hundreds of islands, and each forms a world of its own. On one small island there are four mutually unintelligible languages. In West Camerouns in Africa, a land not as large as Massachusetts, live at least twenty different tribes, each of which speaks its own tongue.

As the gospel spreads throughout the world bringing light and life to the sons of men everywhere, it grows in each piece of the mosaic in a way specially suited to *that* piece. Each homogeneous unit of the population has its own language, thought forms, precious culture, power structure, and political forms. Some units are patriarchal, some matriarchal; some rich, some poor; and some timid and some brave. Furthermore, the Church in each is at a certain stage. Much depends on whether the Church at this moment is composed of 1 percent of the people group or 50 percent of it. A large denomination surging forward victoriously is one thing; a small denomination facing defeat and confusion is another. Each has radically different needs.

Much mission and church work goes astray here. Churches in India feel they are working with Indians or, in Indonesia, with Indonesians; whereas actually each is working with one piece, usually one very small piece, of the Indian or Indonesian mosaic. For example, the Scottish Presbyterians in Nagpur, India, did educational work. They worked with the wealthy, the elite, the rulers and merchants of the city. The mission high school and college touched less than 1 percent of the total population. The elite, as so often is the case, were highly resistant to Christianity. At the end of the first century of labor, the Church gathered by this mission numbered about five hundred communicant Christians. At the same time in the city of Nagpur were two hundred thousand laborers, largely Mahars by caste. These people were receptive to Christianity—but the Church was not working in that receptive piece of the mosaic and had established no Mahar churches.

But more wisely, the Lutherans in Chota Nagpur found many

castes, of which two (the Uraons and Mundas) were receptive. The Lutherans concentrated on these—as did the Roman Catholics who came about forty years later. Today there are at least seven hundred thousand Christians of both Churches, and that part of India is well on the way to becoming largely Christian.

This second basic principle—that major church growth ordinarily takes place in receptive units of the population—has much meaning for the production of Christian literature. To begin with, literature must be indigenous:

> We need tracts redolent with the idiom, names, colour, sociology, religious beliefs, and practices of the citizens of this fair land [the Philippines]. They should mention Rizal, Mabini, and De los Reyes. They should be written by Gonzales, Ibalarossa and Fernandez. They should tell of turning from tuba, cock fighting and gambling, and be illustrated with pictures of carabaos, bananas and coconuts.[2]

What I wrote was a generally recognized and increasingly practiced part of the truth. Literature should be indigenous in that sense. But "indigenous" must mean not merely Filipino; it must mean "being suited to particular parts of the total population"—the Ilocanos, Cebuanos, Isnegs, peasants, or university students. Literature must fit the one part of the mosaic in which it is intended to spread the gospel. It must be couched in the language and thought forms of that piece. It must be filled with names of persons typical of that piece and tell stories about men and women of that segment. In a word, literature for Harlem or Watts must not merely be American, not merely written in English: it must fit Harlem or Watts. It should sound strange and possibly be repugnant to Anglo churches in Boston and Minneapolis. Christian literature overseas has a long way to go to incarnate this principle.

Christian literature should not be talking to everybody about everything. It should be devising specific communications to specific groups in which the Holy Spirit is at work. The obedient steward, as a mark of his obedience, will discern where the finger of God is pointing. The alert servant, as a mark of his faithfulness, will observe when the spirit moves the waters of healing and rush to put the sick man in.

Christian literature should be seeking out those segments of the

2. Ibid., p. 98.

total population which have become responsive and constructing messages about God's grace in ways likely to appeal to those segments. They are our prime prospects. When God plans to bring some people out of Egypt into the freedom of Christ, Christian literature should learn the language, thought forms, and culture of *that people* and construct meticulously stated messages suited to *it*.

Readers will easily apply to literature the following example from the field of radio. In northeast Ghana the Chokosi, a small tribe of twenty-two thousand, in 1964 started to turn to Christ. During the next five years about one thousand of them became Christians in a dozen village churches. The missionary, A. C. Krass, believed that the whole tribe was responsive and could be won by 1980.

Radio messages from the powerful Christian station (ELWA) in Liberia reach these villages with ease. Messages in the trade language about the gospel and the life, death, and resurrection of the Lord Jesus can be heard, but few listen to the trade language. General messages, in a language other than their own, do not move the Chokosi greatly.

But suppose that the mission working there were to sell cheap radios to every headman in every Chokosi hamlet and to prepare messages in Chokosi. Suppose every village elder who has become Christian with his people were to be interviewed and a tape made which sounded even more specific and Chokosi than the following:

> I am Monganga, chief of the village of Chereponi. My mother's people live in Tola. My maternal uncles are Wakeena and Trabee. My daughters are married into the chief's family in Ibadola. We called the missionary to teach us. He came regularly for many months. All the people of my village decided to become Christians together. We built a church, learned how to worship God, were baptized, and are following the Christian way. We want all our relatives to become Christians too. It is a good religion. If you call us, we will come and teach you. I will send my son, who has learned much of the Bible. Do not delay. The Bible says, "Now is the day of salvation." All Chokosi are becoming Christian.

As villages requested instruction, their names would be broadcast. Deaths, sicknesses, recoveries, and news would also be broadcast. Baptisms would be announced over the radio and attended by thousands. A constant stream of tapes would be sent to ELWA for beaming out to this one small segment in all Africa which speaks Chokosi. As the dear heart language came over the air and the Chokosi tribesmen recognized the voices of their relatives, how intently they would listen! Bible teaching and sermons, hymns, and passages to memorize in Chokosi could be broadcast for use by new congregations.

This high degree of specificity (and remember, specific needs are all that exist; general needs are a myth) might reasonably be expected to shorten drastically the time needed to win a tribe to the Christian life. In the old days it took decades to spread the gospel through half a population. Today we should use radio and literature to reach specific homogeneous units and Christianize them by effecting a radical transformation of their lives in a few years. True, radio would only supplement the living and present deacons and elders, preachers and Bible teachers. These would have to be created by the mission concerned.

Obviously literature also can speak to receptive units of the population where a Christward march is on, and can further that one march in every way.

Emphasizing Group Conversion

The third basic principle to be used in Christian literature is that conglomerate churches have difficulty communicating the faith, whereas one-people churches grow much more healthily. Where converts individually are pried out of several social units and added to the Lord, there conglomerate congregations arise. Their members come from many societies. Suppose a conglomerate church is planted in Chicago from these segments of population—Puerto Ricans, Swedish, Irish, black, rich, poor, highly educated, and slightly educated. This kind of a church is born with a weak physique. It requires much care to survive and reproduces with difficulty.

In contrast, churches that grow from people movements (i.e., one-people churches) have a more robust physique and can grow both more rapidly and more soundly. Writers of Christian literature ought always to remember this.

A people movement occurs within one people when a series of groups, each comprising perhaps five families and perhaps fifty, jointly decides to become Christian, while continuing on in their ancestral homes, earning their living in time-honored ways, and remaining in effective contact with their unconverted relatives. When the unconverted, after suitable instruction in the Christian religion by similar group decisions, declare for Christ, renounce all other gods, and become Christians, they further the people movement. Thus over the decades large and strong denominations arise. Often they number hundreds of thousands.

Such people movements have occurred in all the continents and most countries of the world. One thinks immediately of Tseltals of Mexico, Chilean Pentecostals, Javanese Muslims, Ethiopian Wallamos and Kambattas, Kikuyus of Kenya, Malas and Madigas of India, and hundreds of others.

Conglomerate churches grow slowly; people-movement churches have the ability to grow soundly and rapidly. Despite this, Christian literature frequently advocates one-by-one growth leading to the formation of conglomerate churches. Such church planting necessarily proceeds hesitantly in low gear.

Let us get at the matter by asking if the Christian literature you readers know expects one-by-one or family-by-family and group-by-group conversion. Literature will generally get what it expects. Does Christian literature quote those passages of Scripture that seem to require isolated individual action? Or does literature quote those many passages where households become Christian? If one goes through the Book of Acts and underlines each time that a household, a multitude, or a synagogue community or large parts of each of these units became Christian, he soon sees that "group action" was ordinary procedure in the New Testament church. When God took a people out of Egypt, He took twelve tribes—not individuals but tribes. When the synagogue at Berea turned to Christian faith, practically the whole Jewish community converted together.

Do the writers of our Christian literature know the people-movement mode of becoming Christian, know how biblical it is, quote the Bible in describing it, and sometimes subtly and sometimes openly plead that readers move by social units into the glorious liberty of the sons of God? Do readers of Christian literature learn of many converts who have accepted Christ *with* their loved ones? Or does Christian literature convey the impression that to become Christian one must always break away from his family and act in antisocial ways? Does Christian literature encourage the conversion of rebels and those who are already at odds with their clans and families? Or does Christian literature constantly set before men the desirability of acting in concert with loved ones?—while, of course, stating clearly that if loved ones, after being wooed for months or years, will not become Christian together, the one who has deep Christian conviction must act alone, while using every way open to him to keep affectionately related to his as yet unconvinced family members.

Many other principles bear on literature, radio, and church growth. Once missionaries and church leaders recognize these principles, they think biblically and realistically about propagating the gospel. They can communicate the gospel more effectively. They become better stewards of the grace of God. They intuitively determine priorities, apportion budgets more suitably. They see roadblocks more clearly and find ways around them more quickly. Opportunities are more swiftly recognized and developed. Such missionaries and national ministers write more effective tracts, articles, news items, and letters. In short, they have married church-growth theory to the preparation of Christian literature and radio broadcasts.

But frequently costly decisions will be required to turn from one kind of literature to the other. Such turning will not be easy. It will cost time, money, and labor. It will, however, pay rich dividends. Momentous decisions in the right direction in Christian communication are an urgent necessity today.

21

New Urban Faces
of the Church

Roger Greenway of Westminster Theological Seminary is the editor of an influential magazine, *Urban Mission*. He writes, "The highest and best mission leaders often spend more time devising strategies to reach 100 tribal cavemen in some remote corner of earth than to reach the urban millions—apartment house dwellers, slum residents, and new rural-urban migrants—and multiply churches among them." I believe Greenway is substantially correct in this dramatic statement. It is clear that if mission leaders are to reverse this trend, momentous decisions will be required.

New thousands of missionary-minded laymen must be led to see the enormous importance of urban evangelization. The heroism of missionaries who went to remote jungle areas used to be dramatized and did serve effectively in creating thousands of supporters who equated mission with David Livingstone in darkest Africa. Today and tomorrow we must make the momentous decisions required to create multitudes of supporters who see urban mission as the most important missionary work today.

We all recognize that advocates of the effective evangelization of many pieces of the mosaic would all acclaim their piece of the mosaic as the most important work in mission today—and should recognize that each one of them is very important.

With this introductory statement we pass on to a consideration of a view of the multitudinous urban faces of Christian mission today.

The Need for Many New Faces of the Church

Churches must fit the segments of population in which they are multiplying. Each must read the Bible in and worship in the language spoken by its segment. At church suppers each must serve the kind of food that group likes. The pastor must appear to the members and to potential members as "one of us." The house of worship must be one to which Christians can invite their pagan or worldly friends, knowing that they will feel at home there. The expositions of Scripture must speak to the actual inner life of that particular section of the population. If we wish to be effectively evangelistic, we must multiply congregations which, in these and many other ways, fit their segments of the citizenship.

Since urban mankind is a vast mosaic of innumerable pieces, my thesis is that the Church in the cities of the world must have multitudinous new urban faces. A significant part of the plateaued or declining membership of many congregations and denominations is that their image of the church is limited to what it should be like in *their* segments of the urban population.

For example, an upper-middle-class denomination will build and maintain an urban face which suits upper-middle-class people. As, under the command of eternal God to make the gospel known to all pieces of the mosaic, that comfortable denomination works at discipling its hugely growing city, it must expect to create and appear in some new urban faces. Its present face fits upper-middle-class people, and cities have many segments which are not upper middle class. The denomination will develop a new face in each segment it evangelizes effectively.

Let us study the urban mosaic for a few minutes. We shall first look at cities in the United States. This nation is English-speaking, democratic, and prides itself on being a melting pot in which groups of immigrants speaking many languages—German, Swedish, Italian, Spanish, Chinese, French, Rumanian, Russian, Latvian, Greek, Japanese, Filipino, Tagalog, Ilocano, Mono, Kikongo, Ashanti, Hindi, Tsutuhil, and on and on—have been assimilated. Since they now speak English, live in houses with indoor plumbing, and drive cars, we may be sure they are now all one people—Americans. In one very thin sense they are all one people; but it is more realistic to see them as many peoples.

As I was writing this, my phone rang. The caller talked for half an hour concerning the kind of congregation which would meet the needs of the piece of the urban mosaic in which he was working. He found that if he evangelized the gangs made up of fifty or more young men and boys, he would win many converts. If he took them to conventional English-speaking churches, the converts would disappear. If he formed groups of converts into living churches where they felt at home, they stayed. He was developing a new urban face of the Universal Church of Jesus Christ.

At the other end of the scale, a southern Californian minister of a respected small denomination found that if he concentrated his efforts on owners of four-hundred-thousand-dollar houses, a largely unchurched population, he could win them. Most were born Christians but did not attend any church. When they were encouraged to form a congregation, they responded favorably. The church which resulted had much financial power.

These examples give us a glimpse of the multitudinous situations in which churches form, transform sinners into saints, influence their way of life, map out their areas of evangelistic potency, and determine what kinds of mission they will carry out.

These many peoples in the United States exist in a nation dedicated to the dictum that all citizens are equal. All have the vote; none may be paid less than the minimum wage. All Americans are one people! We Americans are proud of our oneness. Equal rights are guaranteed by the Constitution. We shy away from any idea of different ranks in society. Christians carry this feeling a step further. In Christ there is no Jew or Greek, no slave or free, no male or female. Every Christian is equally loved by God and has an equal vote in the Church. The Church fights for brotherhood. All readers of this chapter will feel a Christian hesitancy in believing that the urban mosaic legitimately continues in the Church.

Nevertheless, as they survey their cities, readers will also agree that our cities (and churches) do manifest many different styles of living. The communities in which university professors live are quite different from those in which coal miners are the major element of the population. Congregations in which farm owners are the main members are different from those in which farm laborers and small-town mechanics constitute nine-tenths of the membership.

Congregations made up of first-generation Hispanics, who speak very little English, are different from those made up of fourth-generation Hispanics, who speak little Spanish.

New urban faces of the Church form in this multicolored mosaic. Each group differs from the others in degree of education, amount of income, cost of home, kinds of employment, and a thousand other ways.

Obstacles and Opportunities in Church Growth

Perhaps the greatest obstacle to church growth is the face of the churches so common in America—a splendid building with a five-acre parking lot and many helpful activities carried on by various groups. The more groups there are, the more kinds of people can be served and held in the orbit of the church. This may be called the face of the American urban church. It fits suburban, middle-class communities very well; it does not fit the inner city at all. In the inner cities of the world, congregations must fit the physical, social, economic, and racial characteristics of the segments of population—the *ethnē*—being evangelized.

The most striking example of this may be seen in the churches which multiplied during the first fifty years of the Christian era. They met in homes, rented halls, patios, gardens, and other convenient places. They spent nothing for buildings or upkeep. They never assembled one hundred people for worship. Their assemblies were small gatherings in which everybody knew everybody else.

As immigrants from Puerto Rico streamed into New York City after World War II, the Pentecostal Christians amongst them leaned in the direction of the New Testament churches. They rented small stores on the streets of the city. These were fifteen to eighteen feet wide and sixty feet long. They had a small room or two at the back. When one hundred people came in, the place was crowded. At the Sunday-school hour, teachers sat on the narrow backs of the benches. Each faced a couple of rows of people who formed his class. Often a church would have four classes in that one long, narrow room. The noise was terrific. Such storefront churches were self-supporting. They fitted the way in which the poverty-stricken Puerto Ricans lived. Scores, perhaps hundreds, of such churches were founded. The unemployed, poor, shaken men and women from Puerto Rico were a hugely receptive segment of humanity. Had the missionary societies of North America recognized and reproduced this urban face of the church, a mighty harvest would have been reaped. Instead they too frequently opened social-service institutions that did little to multiply churches suitable to this population.

Obedient Pragmatism

As urban missions of all denominations, from Friends to Roman Catholics, set about discipling urban multitudes, they must be obediently pragmatic. They must not, of course, be pragmatic in regard to eternal truth revealed in the Bible. They must be pragmatic as to what urban face of the Church fits the piece of the mosaic to which God sends them, to disciple it and teach it to observe all things our Lord has commanded us.

Is this pragmatic approach pleasing to God? If it is obedient to the Bible, filled with the Holy Spirit, feels comfortable to the Christian citizens of that segment of society, and *works*, then it is pleasing to God. The key principle here is that voiced in Romans 16:25—eternal God has *commanded* that the gospel be made known to all pieces of the human mosaic *(panta ta ethnē)* to bring them to faith and obedience. If a given way of evangelizing does not bring men and women of that piece of the mosaic to faith and obedience, it thwarts God's command. That way of preaching, worshiping, evangelizing, and living must be adjusted until it does bring members of that *ethnos* to faith and obedience. God commands it. That way is pleasing to Him. We want new urban faces which God does bless to the winning of sinners of *panta ta ethnē* to faith and obedience.

The ways we work and worship must be *effective* in bringing members of each segment of society to saving faith in Christ and responsible membership in His Body. This principle has been overlooked by many denominations in this and other lands. The needs of human beings are many and clamant—destitute children, abandoned women, hungry people, oppressed minorities, destitute elderly, youth who roam the streets, and so on. Each of these groups has physical, educational, emotional, and economic needs which charitable Christians feel they must meet. Consequently they engage in urban work which, while meeting many highly visible needs, fails to feed starving souls. It does not give away the Bread of Heaven.

I am thinking of a "Church of All Peoples" in a great eastern city.

Over the past fifty years this church has spent more than five million dollars and has an institutional presence on three acres of very costly urban soil. It has rendered tremendous service of one kind and another to multitudes of immigrants. But the single church it has planted is made up of the staff of the institution with sixty-three others, only thirty-eight of whom live in the vicinity. It has not brought the many *ethnē* it has served to faith and obedience. New urban faces of the Church must be multipliers of biblical ongoing congregations of the saved. Urban "work" must never be substituted for urban "mission." The word *mission* must be reserved for the conscious effort—including all kinds of charitable work—to bring sinners to repentance and faith and to build them into soundly Christian, reproductive congregations.

Effective Faces of the Urban Churches

Faces always have noses. These come in a variety of forms—upturned, saucy, Roman, broad, narrow, hooked. The nose is a prominent part of the face. So is the leadership pattern of a church. Today the common leadership pattern is for all the ministers of the Church to be highly educated. That this pattern was not manifested in the New Testament churches, where to Jewish rabbis the leaders of the Church seemed to be "uneducated and untrained men" (Acts 4:13), makes little difference to us. "Today," we say, "ministers in our denomination must be seminary graduates. We are a respectable church." This leadership pattern (this nose) fits one kind of face. It does not fit many others.

If churches are to grow and multiply (and they will have to do that if urban masses are to be discipled), then the leaders, the ministers of those churches will have to be perceptibly men of the masses, each of whom feels quite at home in his segment of the urban population. If we are thinking of Hispanic millions in America, we must recognize that the Hispanic mosaic has many pieces. First-generation Hispanics can be seen as multitudes of factory workers, unemployed, day laborers, and the like. They will not be effectively addressed by men who have passed through high school, college, and three years of seminary training. That kind of education will *un*fit them for effective harvesting in these ripe fields. A high thin Roman nose does not look right in a congregation made up of people with upturned, saucy noses. The face must fit the forming congregation. A leadership pattern which fits the segment of population which has been discipled (enrolled) is the first of four faces which I describe.

The second is equally important. The church appears as a cluster of "house churches." This face is being seen more and more in many countries.

In São Paulo, Brazil, I visited an Assemblies Church of more than six thousand members. Its building seated only seven hundred. "How," I asked, "could six thousand be served by such a small building?" The pastor replied, "In addition to this, we have 207 churches." "How many of these are rented halls and empty sheds?" I inquired. "Thirty-seven," he replied. "And the rest?" "They are homes," he said. "All my house-church people come here when they have need. Every Sunday this church is full."

That urban face fitted that section of São Paulo made up of poor, often unemployed Brazilians. They had become Christians in house churches, where each knew all the others and all felt completely at home. The pastor and his assistants and the leaders of the 207 house churches were themselves working-class migrants from northeast Brazil. These leaders were continually establishing new house churches by splitting one into two or by encouraging new believers to form new house churches.

The house church of today is seldom like those in the New Testament, which had no central building at all. Today there is generally a central building, tabernacle, or large rented hall. This central congregation led by a full-time pastor encourages the formation of many Christian cells or Bible-study and worship groups. These are expected to function as full churches. In a few cases the unpaid leader of the group celebrates Communion with his small flock. In most cases Communion is observed in the central building once a month or once a quarter.

Most ministers in America and most missionaries regard the degree of Christian instruction given in house churches and the worship experienced in them as deplorably low in quality. However, it appears sufficient to hold large numbers of city dwellers in the Christian orbit, to give them at least some biblical teaching, and to lead many to genuine faith in Christ.

Another example of the multiplication of house churches comes from the town of Eagle Rock, just west of Pasadena, California. There a Christian Assembly, affiliated with the Four Square Church, in 1975 had a membership of three hundred and worshiped in a small well-built church. Its pastor, Donald Pickerill, decided to "decentral-ize." He formed thirty house churches, each led by a priest. Each church met in the homes of its ten members. These knew each other well and resided close to each other. Once a month five contiguous churches would meet as a company of fifty in some home with a large front room. By 1979 the membership had grown to eight hundred. There were now seventy functioning house churches. Meetings at the central church also continued.

I asked Pickerill, "When are you going to build a bigger church?" "Never!" he answered. "We believe that in today's cities 'house churches' lead to a more actually Christian way of life than the 'one-big-building' form. However," he went on, "we have not grown in the past three years. We are still at eight hundred. We must find ways to get going again."

Indeed they must. The house churches, being free of the need to build expensive sanctuaries, theoretically have no limits to growth. The Full Gospel Church on Yoido Island, Seoul, Korea, now has more than one hundred thousand members. Its thousands of house churches are multiplying in all parts of that great urban area. Growth there is greatly assisted by the central church, which seats nine thousand and occupies the most visible church site in Korea. The pastor, Paul Yonggi Cho, an eloquent speaker and organizational genius, is aided by a full-time paid staff of more than sixty. "But," he was careful to emphasize, "the unpaid leaders of our thousands of house churches (more than half of them women; they are more compassionate than men) are the most essential part of our church."

The third new urban face of the Church is made up of churches, all in one highly responsive segment of the urban population. This face is usually produced by powerful purposeful missionary effort.

A fine example is found in the city of Madras. There a small denomination, the Evangelical Church of India, fathered by the Oriental Missionary Society, found a highly responsive segment of urban society and, for the past fifteen years, has been multiplying churches in it. Membership has zoomed from one thousand to more than twelve thousand. The new Christian urbanites have said to their country relatives, "You also ought to become Christians," and in that segment of society, village churches also have sprung up.

The plan of evangelization is as follows. The church-cum-mission recruits several evangelistic teams, primarily from the high-school-educated young men of this segment. These teams locate communities of their people in which churches might be started and hold evangelistic campaigns there for one to three weeks, depending on response. Men and women deciding to follow Christ are baptized and formed into ongoing congregations, which for a while meet in convenient places. As soon as it is certain that a church is going to result, the church-cum-mission purchases a small piece of land—perhaps twenty-five by forty feet in size. On it is erected a one-room brick church building. (The funding—two or three thousand dollars per church—is raised in America.) The building gives this congregation a permanent gleaming white house of worship. It gives the Christians status. It assures regular worship.

The best of the team members are sent on to seminary, and thus a constant supply of well-trained pastors—*of the people*—is assured. Currently the Evangelical Church expects to plant a church a week in India, many of them in Madras City and its burgeoning environs.

The fourth new face of the church is that seen in the millions of migrants to new lands. These are frequently highly responsive. There are scores of such migrant minorities, each presenting a unique opportunity to carry out eternal God's command to bring all *ethnē* to faith and obedience.

The face assumed in each migrant multitude will be different. The Cambodian refugees on the eastern side of Thailand, while still refugees, built the largest congregation and largest church building in all Thailand. That is unusual. Most faces will be some form of house churches or rented halls or cheap temporary structures, with central buildings going up as Christians multiply. If the economy prospers as Christians multiply, they erect big church buildings. In most cities, however, Christianity spreads among the proletariat, and costly buildings are not a part of the new face.

Let me now mention a few opportunities for churches to multiply in urban migrant minorities. Twenty-five years ago a Roman Catholic priest in Italy, who had espoused the biblical faith and come to America, said to me,

All across Canada in the big cities are tens of thousands of recent Italian immigrants. These are mostly from Italy's country districts. The men are intensely anticlerical. Many are believing Marxists; but this faith seems to wane on getting to Canada. If any missionary society in

America would throw half a dozen missionary families into this ripe
and responsive segment of humanity, it could soon plant dozens of
congregations of soundly believing Christians. This is a spiritually-
starving half million.

Subsequent inquiries in Canada have led me to believe that my
informant was correct. Of course, the missionaries would have to
learn both standard Italian and the dialect of Italian spoken by the
immigrants from each particular section of Italy. Small groups of ten
to twenty Christians, meeting in rented halls or on Sunday morning in
empty bars, could be formed. With help from the founding missionary organization, permanent places of worship could be obtained, and
what the Oriental Missionary Society has done in Madras could be
duplicated here among a very different kind of people.

The Reverend Dan Kelly is a Canadian missionary to the American
Indians. When studying at the School of World Mission in Pasadena,
he surveyed the American Indian population in the sprawling Los
Angeles metropolitan area. He found that there are more than one
hundred thousand American Indians in the area, of whom fewer than
one thousand are in church on Sunday. Ninety-nine thousand unchurched American Indians live here! Nothing could possibly be done
for them which would more quickly elevate their character and status
than for thousands of them to become Bible-believing and obeying
Christians. If they are invited to join existing white churches, they will
decline. In them they will not feel at home. But if some denomination
or missionary society would plant six hundred Indian churches
among them, then perhaps sixty thousand would become responsible
members. Six thousand dedicated Indians would become leaders.
They would carry back to their relatives on the reservations the good
news that when you obey and worship Him, Christ redeems and
elevates.

I was in a church a year ago where the pastor told the congregation,
"There are more Samoans in California than there are in Samoa. We
are recalling our missionary to Samoa and asking him to multiply
congregations of Samoans in California." I have not checked the
number of Samoans in this state, but since there are thousands of
Vietnamese and Thais, hundreds of thousands of Filipinos and
Koreans, and millions of Hispanics, I see no reason to doubt his
statement.

Cubans, Haitians, Portuguese, Turks, and many others in America constitute scores of distinct segments of humanity. Some are more responsive than others. In most there are subsections. Thus the first-generation Mexican immigrants are highly responsive if properly approached. Fourth-generation Hispanics are less responsive; but if won, they present fewer problems as they multiply congregations.

This face of the Church resembles that of the tens of thousands of Pentecostal Puerto Ricans who, in the fifties, worshiped in storefronts in New York and other cities. The aiding missionary society may be able to help the multiplying indigenous churches to house themselves permanently. But where the groups worship is a secondary matter. The primary matter is that in a responsive unit of humanity hundreds of congregations, by God's grace, are established.

I recently visited Japan and lectured on church growth to a gathering of pastors from many of the great cities of that nation. A highly perceptive missionary expounded at some length on the fact that in Japan the men live in many sections of the city; but they leave those sections every morning to go to their company and do not return until late at night. The corporate life at the company, the fellowship of other employees, and the social times there make that the most meaningful group in the life of most Japanese men. The company is their income, their work, their comradeship, and their life. The pastors discussed this concept with considerable agreement. Were a group of believers to form in that most meaningful group at the place of work, it would be natural and influential. It would certainly be a new urban face of the Church. It might reach back into the homes and form subcongregations there!

New urban faces of the Church will all have one feature in common. All will be composed of persons who have heard the gospel, believed it, obeyed Christ, and become responsible members of His Body. But the faces of that Body will be multifarious. As land gets more and more costly, few faces will look like a beautiful suburban sanctuary with a five-acre parking lot. As gasoline runs out forty years from now, many small humble places of worship will be seen. Worshipers will walk to them. The Lord will find hungering pieces of the human mosaic and in them will multiply gatherings of believers. Through these He will distribute the bread of heaven. The Church will spread through the lower ranks of society. We shall then look back with amazement at the time when the most orthodox churches were those composed of the most prosperous citizens.

The Church will not transform all segments of humanity into one homogeneous unit, all of whose members speak Esperanto, English, or Hindi. The Bible tells us that on that great day men from every tribe, nation, people, and tongue will be before the throne. As the Church spreads throughout the unbelievably complex fabric of urban mankind, it will assume many faces. Each is an urban face of His Body, the Church.

22

Withdrawing Missionaries— Right or Wrong?

Withdrawing missionaries has become fashionable. One society after another announces that it is reducing the number of its overseas workers. The dean of a missionary training school in the United States writes, "Perhaps one of the greatest acts of charity that missionary societies will be called on to perform during this decade is the withdrawal of the financial support and missionary personnel now used abroad." From some fields missionaries may be phased out largely and from others entirely.

Leading spokesmen of the missionary enterprise declare that dealings with their younger Churches (which, to them, is what missions have come to be) can be carried out more satisfactorily by occasional visits of an administrator than by maintaining a corps of long-term missionaries. Some boards have taken the grave step of ceasing to appoint long-term missionaries. Appointments are now made of American ministers and specially qualified laymen for one brief term of service overseas.

The outcome of these trends can be seen in mission statistics. For instance, one North American communion reports the numbers of missionaries sent to an important Latin American country as ninety-six in 1952 and thirty in 1968, and today there are fewer than ten. True, during the postwar years many boards increased the number of

191

missionaries they sent and are now maintaining those numbers at high levels. Some are actually increasing them. On the whole, the last quarter century has seen a definite trend toward withdrawing more and more of Christ's ambassadors overseas. Consequently, I ask, "Is withdrawing right or wrong?"

Some associations of missionary societies are affected more than others. Those affiliated with the Division of Overseas Ministries of the National Council of the Churches of Christ show the most pronounced reductions. But a leading conservative board in 1957 had 571 missionaries in Nigeria. The World Christian Encyclopedia of 1982 says there are fewer than 400.

The isolationist mood in the United States which the Vietnam War initiated on such a large scale—so sedulously encouraged by world communism and all its hidden fronts—influences the mood in missions. It should not, but it does. People who hold this view ask, "Why carry these burdens? It is really better for Asians if we get out. They don't want us. Their leaders will do better if we are gone. Leave Asia to the Asians." Whether or not such sentiments are justified in the colossal military and political struggle now raging is one thing; whether they are justified in God's program of world evangelization is an entirely different thing.

Part of the setting is that the missionary has taken a beating. During the past decades, enemies have assaulted him. Non-Christians—secularists, Marxists, Hindus, Jews, and others who do not believe the gospel and do not want it propagated—have sharply criticized missions. They have described missionaries as stupid, arrogant, and no longer needed. Even some missionaries who served overseas for a few months or years, needing to justify that they are not returning to their fields, have alleged "failure and follies" on the part of those who remained on the field.

Friends also have criticized the missionary. Better ways of missionizing, more effective methods of helping young Churches, smoother ways of working with men and women of other cultures, and more sensitivity to interpersonal relationships needed to be instituted. This involved naming the mistakes missionaries were making. The gleaming image conjured up in the mind of the ardent Christian by the word *missionary* has of late—particularly in some quarters—lost much of its luster. If the need of the three billion for Christ, if the continued multiplication of cells of Christians everywhere does not soon regain that luster, it is going to be increasingly difficult for men to hear God's call to world evangelization. For some denominations withdrawal seems likely to become irreversible.

Financial stringency and declining income for missionary societies cannot be considered real reasons for reduction of the missionary force. They are no doubt responsible for some current pulling out. Certain boards have been de-emphasizing evangelism. Many supporters, not liking this, are giving to other causes. Such boards are suffering a sharp reduction in income and are cutting down their missionary staff. If they would stress church-multiplying missions in unchurched sections of cities and countrysides abroad, their income would bounce back up. America has not grown poor. Its gross national product is greater than ever. The Lord's arm has not been shortened. He has not revoked the Great Commission. If a missionary society turns from evangelism and suffers decline of income, we must not believe lack of money is a basic reason for withdrawal of missionaries.

To be sure, it is quite possible for a vigorously evangelistic missionary society, suffering financial reverses, *temporarily* to decrease its number of missionaries. But, as it does so, it hardens its resolve to reconcile men of every tribe and tongue to God-in-Christ, and to increase its number of missionaries as soon as possible. It courageously recruits lifetime missionaries, gives them the best training possible, and sends them out with prayer to bring the peoples of earth to the obedience of the faith. Such a society knows that the great days of the missionary enterprise lie ahead. It will be missionizing vigorously a hundred years from now—if the Lord tarries. The great turnings from Confucianism, animism, Islam, and Hinduism have yet to come. A slightly leaner force for a few years due to temporary financial stringencies is not the same thing at all as withdrawal of missionaries because a society judges that the day of missions is over. Both reductions may coincide with a business recession, but they are radically different phenomena.

Why Societies Withdraw Missionaries

Withdrawing missionaries has in some quarters become fashionable in the past few years—but is it right? The biblical answer is simple: to the extent that withdrawing missionaries retards or hinders the evangelization of the three billion who have yet to believe—or worse, is dictated by a conviction that world evangelization is an unworthy goal—withdrawing is wrong.

To the extent that it is a temporary tack—a skillful shifting of direction to meet a change of wind—withdrawing is right. If it is based on a judgment that the destination will be reached faster by sailing away from it for a while, withdrawing is justified. The Church and her missionary societies must hold steadily in view the ultimate goal for which the Lord Christ died and rose again. Progress is to be measured by advancement toward that end. Deviations in direction—if they are not betrayals of the cause—are either zigzags calculated to gain the goal more certainly or unavoidable defeats. It is not permissible to substitute other and "better" goals. There is no better goal than that men come to love and obey Jesus Christ and by His grace live as responsible members of His Body. Every other good goal can be more effectively achieved by men and women who are practicing Christians continually under the command of their Head.

Ministers and laymen must not simply acquiesce in withdrawals. They must judge whether they are tragic defeats, temporary tactical moves which promise more rapid and effective evangelization of the three billion, faithless abandonment of the Great Commission (substituting other "more urgent" or "more relevant" goals is the way in which abandonment is often proposed), or entirely justifiable redeployment. Let us examine some historic withdrawals of each variety.

First, consider the withdrawals of missionaries from China, North Korea, and Nagaland. These were defeats. The first two, forced by communist governments, were beyond the power of the Church to avoid. The third was inflicted by a friendly nation, tens of thousands of whose students each year are welcomed into the universities of England, America, Germany, Sweden, Australia, and other lands where Christian Churches are strong. Whether the expulsion of missionaries from Nagaland was sufficiently protested and the access given to Hindu and Muslim missionaries to western nations was sufficiently argued, I do not know; but the sealing off of any segment of humanity from missionary labors is a backward step. It denies religious liberty. It withholds knowledge of the Savior from those hungering for Him. It may have to be endured; it should never be accepted. It should be counted a tragic defeat.

Second, consider the withdrawals from most of their fields which have been carried out by several great missionary societies. In 1950 they had twice as many missionaries abroad as in 1980. They intend further reductions. What shall we say about such withdrawals? Are they temporary tactical moves or ruthless abandonment of the task?

These withdrawals are commonly defended on two grounds. The first is that governments no longer welcome missionaries; the sending churches must realize that in this postcolonial era numbers of missionaries will be small. This is faulty reasoning. Governments have seldom welcomed missionaries. William Carey was kept out of India for years. Until 1890 most South American governments vigorously excluded Protestant missionaries. How determined an effort to persuade governments have societies made? How does it happen that other missionary societies have succeeded in getting their missionaries in? If missionaries are prevented from entering closed Country X, why have they not been sent to open Country Y? If a given missionary society has several fields, a hostile government might force it out of one, but why should its missionaries not be deployed in others?

The second defense is that churches can do the job better and missions should turn work over to them. One board says, "The Church of 9,170 communicants we have planted can now carry on. Its national leaders can do the work better than American missionaries. All our schools are now manned by nationals. All the congregations have indigenous pastors. Almost all nurses, doctors, and technicians in our hospitals are nationals. We once had eighty missionaries and now have seventeen; but these seventeen assist a Church in which 171 employed nationals and a host of volunteers are continually at work. Reducing the missionaries and increasing the work is good stewardship. After all, we are here to establish the Church. This we have done. It is time to withdraw and let the Church carry on." What shall we say to this common argument?

Obviously, transferring authority to nationals these days is an expedient move. Usually it is also a good move. There can be no disagreement here. But, bearing the Great Commission in mind, one must ask, "How large a section of the country is that denomination of 9,170 communicants evangelizing?" Let us be under no misapprehensions. Most daughter denominations in the third world are rather small. The median denomination (cluster of congregations) in Asia, Africa, or Latin America has a total membership of fewer than one thousand to five thousand scattered in about thirty to one hundred congregations. Some denominations of fifty thousand or one hundred thousand can be found, but they are not common.

Transferring authority to new denominations (large and small) is expedient, but only begins world evangelization. The missionary society must not rest content with making each young Church self-supporting, self-governing, and self-propagating. That is good, but it is not enough. The society must go on to ask, "How large a section of the country is this denomination likely to evangelize?"

For instance, one large American denomination of 1.5 million communicants has planted a sister denomination of 4,201 in one of India's thirteen provinces. The young Church runs itself reasonably well and in a recent year baptized 196 persons. Of these, 181 were children of Christian parents. Only 15 were from "the world." In short, the young Church was doing little effective evangelism. By no flight of the imagination could anyone maintain that the evangelization of India was being accomplished by withdrawing missionaries from India and putting nationals in charge.

In this huge resistant population a very small denomination has been firmly established. It will continue. Most of its children will become Christians. It will evangelize its neighbors as much as most American denominations evangelize theirs. Yet even if it doubles every twenty years, it will be only seventeen thousand strong in 2011—in the midst of a population of at least twenty million.

The mission concerned, staffed by earnest Christians, has, with the best of intentions, been using methods which always produce inch-by-inch growth. The mission needs to move its missionaries to fresh areas (possibly in untouched parts of the twenty million, possibly to more receptive parts of India or some other country) and begin to use effective methods to propagate the gospel.

The Church concerned, going forward now under its own leaders, wasting no time in adjustment to missionary leaders, also should seek to multiply churches. What must not be done is for the American missionary society, having transferred leadership of this tiny Church to nationals, to leave India. To leave is irresponsible. For example, suppose this denomination of 4,201 had been evangelizing its neighbors vigorously and had baptized not 15 from the world but 515. Would this have justified the missionary society in decreasing its "special messengers" from eighty to seventeen? In other parts of that one province, receptive populations can easily be found in which no gospel at all is being proclaimed. Outside that region are twelve other populous regions in which at least two hundred million souls never hear the name of Christ.

How can any missionary society in any country reduce its total number of missionaries as long as three billion live and die without any knowledge of the Savior? How can any missionary society decrease its global sendings on the specious plea that it has turned over authority to one national Church of 4,201—or for that matter, of 804,201?

Third, consider the withdrawals of missionaries from disappointing mission fields. In the glorious expansion of the Christian faith not every mission meets with success. Perhaps twenty missionaries have died of disease or have been sent home broken in health. Perhaps a resistant population has stubbornly rejected the gospel for forty years. Perhaps a young Church (rightly or wrongly) has gotten so angry at its missionary founders that further sendings will simply exacerbate the situation. So the mission is discontinued. For example, miles deep in the forests of Mandala District in India, I visited an abandoned Anglican mission station. The church building, missionary residence, school, and workers' dwellings were falling down. What about such withdrawals?

These are usually defensible. Such "failure" is the price of advance and the vindication of heroism. Mission stations are expendable. Missionary societies, when they attempt great things for God, have no assurance of success. Many mission stations do not succeed, urgent work calls elsewhere, populations move away, and church buildings are put to other uses or torn down. Furthermore, missionaries withdrawn from such fields have usually been sent to others—so really have not been withdrawn at all! Transfer of missionaries from China to Taiwan, Thailand, or Indonesia was justifiable redeployment, not withdrawal. The missionary societies which reinvested their China missionaries in 1948 have clean hands. It is those who took the occasion to reduce their total missionary sendings which have some explaining to do.

Missionary Societies and Young Churches: Partners in Evangelism

The significant Whitby meeting of the International Missionary Council in 1947 coined a notable missionary slogan: Partners in Obedience. The western missionary society and the third-world denomination it was assisting were held to be equal partners. Each had its own obedience to God. Each was to give the other freedom to do the right as God gave it to see the right. Both were partners in obedience to God.

Third-world Churches have insisted that missions turn over authority (and purse strings) to them. This was a necessary move which for the most part has been completed. Third-world Churches (denominations) are now in charge of their own households. Quite properly this has involved a diminution of missionaries in the areas and populations served by those denominations.

It is crucial that younger Churches and their assisting missionary societies estimate correctly what "areas and populations" are adequately served and evangelized by them. Within those areas the young Church should be in charge. After the turning over has been completed, tremendous populations will yet remain unchurched and unevangelized.

Young Churches must not keep missions out of areas and populations they themselves are not evangelizing. Dog-in-the-manger comity is to be avoided at all costs. No young denomination of thirty-four thousand communicants—in the state of Spiritu Santo, Brazil, for example—ought to say or would want to say, "Because we are here in this province of many millions, our fathering mission must not work anywhere in this state. True, we have no plans to evangelize the millions here, but nevertheless our fathering mission must not set foot among them."

On the contrary, the young Church will want to welcome missionaries to multiply churches either in close partnership or in independence out beyond the wards, counties, valleys, plains, or mountains where the denomination has its congregations. The young Church cannot determine the missionary society's "obedience." Partnership in obedience means freedom of both partners to obey God. Young Churches should rejoice that missions go on to father many other clusters of congregations among the three billion who have yet to believe.

Possibly some third-world Churches argue, "If the mission turns over to us and greatly reduces the missionary force which assists us, and keeps sending us a large number of dollars, it will be good for us. Most of the resources we will use for the benefit of the existing congregations, but we shall do some evangelism here and there too." Any such argument is shortsighted. When the American Church ceases to send missionaries, its dedicated men and women will move to other Christian works in the United States or lands which welcome missionaries. And they will pull their money with them. Young Churches will not receive large numbers of dollars after missionaries are assigned to other tasks.

I have been writing as if the sending Churches were exclusively western. This is not the case. Third-world Churches quite commonly send missionaries to other lands and cultures and soon will send many more. Western Churches should rejoice in this, but must remember that all the sendings of eastern and western Churches combined do not begin to match tomorrow's need and opportunity.

A businessman was talking about the evangelization of the northern territories of Ghana. "Why," he asked, "do not the Methodist, Presbyterian, and Anglican denominations of the southern half of Ghana (where perhaps a fifth of the people are Christian) send one thousand Ghanaian missionaries up to the northern territories?"

"Why," I countered, "do not the 2 million Baptists in Texas send two thousand missionaries to evangelize the 2.5 million Spanish-surnamed Americans in Texas whose knowledge of Christ is so slight?" Strong western denominations must not expect weak young denominations (half of whose members are often slightly literate or even illiterate) to do twenty times as much as themselves.

To withdraw missionaries from whole countries and whole continents on the ground that "the duty of the missionary is to work himself out of a job" is to betray a trust. The missionary must, to be sure, work himself out of a job in one township; but he and his board and his supporters must remember that thousands of other townships, counties, cities, areas, and populations full of people who have not yet accepted the name of the Savior await his coming. For the foreseeable future, tasks waiting to be done are very much more numerous than those successfully completed.

Americans spent twenty billion dollars last year for alcoholic drinks. Expenditures for cosmetics and dog food, televisions and pleasure boats, carpets and drapes, skiing and professional football are at an all-time high. This is no time for withdrawing missionaries, cutting back on service, and diminishing the number of mission hospitals and schools. Missionary sendings should mount every year. Some denominations send one missionary for every hundred communicant members. If the ten-million-member United Methodist Church were to follow this proportion, it would send one hundred thousand missionaries. The three billion who have yet to believe could then be divided up into one hundred thousand companies of twenty thousand

and a Methodist missionary assigned to each! The size of the task and the need of the world are stupendous. Withdrawing missionaries in the face of vast and mounting human need cannot be pleasing to God.

It is especially wrong when we recognize that during the last three decades of the twentieth century there are more winnable men and women than there ever have been before. For the first time in history, more than one hundred thousand Muslims have recently become Christians. For the first time in history from 4 to 10 percent of the population of several Asiatic countries have become Christian. For the first time in history a huge continent (Africa south of the Sahara) is becoming substantially Christian during a single century.

We now know enough about cultures in unreached people groups to shepherd the first converts and build them into ongoing churches. We appreciate other cultures as we never have before and shall make sure that Christianity, as it spreads, enhances the cultural treasures of every tribe and tongue. We have learned to work far more harmoniously with Christians of other persuasions, so that loss due to rivalries and disagreements between denominations and missionary societies is at an all-time low.

This is a time to multiply, not to withdraw missionaries. This is a time to pray that God will call our best sons and best daughters to be missionaries. This is the day and the hour for every church, denomination, and society in every continent to magnify missionary sendings, to train appointees better, and to give veterans the best advanced education in missions. The last years of the twentieth century call not for retreat, but for advance in missions!

23

Fragmenting or Upbuilding the Body

Theory and theology of mission must deal with the questions of winning nominal Christians of one branch of the Church into another branch and of starting new churchly associations—new bands of Christians, new denominations, new units of *shalom*. Initiating new programs based on these theological convictions will in some cases require costly and painful decisions. But if they are in the will of God, they will benefit His Church.

Free interplay of persuasion on the basis of the authority and inspiration of the Scripture will work for those denominations which are fervent and obedient, and against those which are not. In this world of thousands of denominations, God uses such free persuasion to renew and revive His Churches. The Reformation renewed the Roman Church. The derided "fundamentalistic" missions and Churches of Latin America—and not the ecumenical movement— have been the most powerful factor in the remarkable (but limited) renewal of the Roman Catholic Church there. The secession of congregations and individuals from any denomination operates powerfully to lead it to meditate on its ways and, if needed, to recall it to its Master and Savior.

True, free persuasion can be and often is misused. Unedifying competition for members and ministers is reprehensible. Some denominations in the United States recruit a large percent of their ministers from "converts" from other denominations—and seldom ask whether higher salary scales and lush fringe benefits play a determining part in the "conversion." Millionaires excommunicated for adultery in strict denominations easily become members of lax denominations.

In Africa and Asia some people movements to Christ have been ruined by Roman Catholics, Adventists, and other denominations rushing in to capture the harvest. Nevertheless, despite this misuse, freedom is good. To see how good it is, one has only to imagine the situation resulting from lack of freedom. Suppose, for example, the Churches were to rule—as the castes in India do—that one is born into them, and the greatest sin of all is to change one's hereditary denomination. The resulting stagnation, complacency of ministers and people alike, formalism, loss of initiative, absence of innovation, and the speedy quenching of those heated in revival can scarcely be exaggerated. The greater the lack of freedom, the greater the stagnation.

The biblical injunction to use freedom wisely must be applied. "You were called to freedom, brethren; only do not use your freedom as an opportunity for the flesh, but through love be servants of one another" (Gal. 5:13, RSV). The words were written to two quarreling parties in the churches of Galatia, but apply on many levels. Freedom is good. Those who do the stagnant sections of the Roman Catholic Church in Latin America most good are not the professional ecumenicists who exhort Protestants to love all Roman Catholics, but those who create living congregations out of those whom the Roman Catholic Church for four hundred years has been content to leave as nominal members. Those who do any stagnant denomination (Roman or evangelical) most good are those who create units of *shalom*, units of Christ's Body, gathered congregations out of the "born Christians," nominals, and marginal adherents. These vital *ecclesiae* may be created inside the stagnant denomination, as Campus Crusade and other organizations attempt to do. They may also—legitimately and blamelessly—be created outside it. Helping congregations become vital is good. Creating vital congregations in existing denominations is good. Creating vital congregations in a new denomination is good.

The Church of Jesus Christ owes a tremendous debt to those who have loved Him so devotedly that they have left the safe shelter of some respectable and somnolent denomination (Chinese, Greek, German,

English, or American) and formed a new fellowship—a gathered church of those who deliberately intend to be Christ's disciples and seek to be filled with His Spirit.

I beg our brothers in the ecumenical wing of the Church to cease pouring scorn on the gathered churches who hold their convictions with such intensity that they remain separate and exclusive. It is not enough for the ecumenical movement to honor and include gathered churches which broke away from parent denominations 150 years ago and now regard their original ardency as schism and sin. The ecumenical movement—to be really ecumenical—should welcome all who love Christ as Lord and Savior according to the Scriptures. Our ecumenical brothers should cease fracturing the Body of Christ by ruling out of it reform movements which feel called of God to separate themselves. The ardent denominations (scornfully called schismatics and sects) are no more separatistic than the Calvinists and Lutherans in the sixteenth century or the Franciscans and Dominicans in earlier times.

Victor Hayward writes, "As regards the fragmentation of Protestantism, I was increasingly appalled at the number of evangelical Christians [90 percent of all Protestants in Latin America] who seem to think they can be the Church of Jesus Christ while paying no attention to their fellow-Christians."[1]

In a similar vein Edward F. Murphy, advocating the organization of new urban congregations in the working-class barrios of the great Latin American cities, writes,

> All converts should immediately be organized into indigenous local churches. These must be brought into a living relationship with the other evangelical churches found in the area. To hold them aloof from the rest of Christ's Body is a violation of Scripture, a sin against God, and evidence of spiritual pride and sectarianism.[2]

These well-spoken words voice a part of the truth. Certainly a sense of the whole body of Christ is a part of being Christian. Yet one cannot forget Paul's stern demand that the Galatian Christians regard themselves as utterly other than the Judaizers who hold to a different

1. Victor Hayward, "Latin America—An Ecumenical Bird's Eye View," *International Review of Missions* 60 (April 1971): 165.
2. Edward F. Murphy, "Opportunities and Guidelines for Urban Evangelization," p. 6.

gospel, pervert the gospel, and are accursed. Yet the Judaizers were baptized Christians in excellent standing in the mother church at Jerusalem. Neither can one forget that had the Franciscans not formed themselves into a distinct and very separate order, the rare insights of Francis would have proved ephemeral indeed. And had the small group of reformers led by John Knox quickly established genial relationships with the rest of the Church led by Mary Queen of Scots and her clergy. . . . But why labor the point? Honest separatism motivated by a desire to incarnate pure devotion to Jesus Christ has played a most significant part in that constant reformation of the Church which marks it off so clearly from the great ethnic religions of mankind. The ecumenical movement—to be really ecumenical— should include both those who are willing to cooperate with the World Council of Churches and those who refuse to. It should count them all Christian. Ecumenicists should perhaps be especially respectful toward those who, in order to hold their doctrine pure, stay aloof from the multitude of cooperating denominations.

Can we not be really ecumenical? Can we not allow and indeed encourage such freedom in the Body of Christ that Christian orders and fervent denominations and exclusive Churches are all counted validly Christian provided only that they accept Jesus Christ as God and Savior and the Bible as the authoritative revealed Word of God? Why impose on others our own standard of toleration? Maybe God has taught them something different.

Our ecumenical brothers do not read the Roman Catholic Church out of the Body because it systematically converts Protestants to Roman Catholicism whenever it can. Why then scorn conservative evangelicals for converting Roman Catholics and mainline Protestants? Could it be that our conciliar brethren, swayed by the power and riches of the Church of Rome, despise the weakness and poverty of the new fervent branches of the Church Universal? And why are some European ecumenicals, who are so tolerant of the five thousand new African denominations, so cool toward the few dozen new thoroughly biblical American denominations? Is it because they are American?

Not all the intolerance is on the side of the conciliar denominations. Can evangelical denominations allow such freedom in the Body of Christ that "culture Churches" (which have ceased to excommunicate members for fault) may be counted as validly Christian, provided only that they accept Jesus Christ as God and Savior and the Bible as the authoritative revealed Word of God? Why impose on others precisely our own understanding of biblical obedience? Maybe the Holy Spirit really teaches them something different from what we believe He teaches us. Our evangelical brothers do not read the Friends out of the Body of Christ for cooperating in a city-wide evangelistic campaign. Why then read the ecumenicists out for including in their fellowship some for whose theological convictions they (the ecumenicists) have scant respect? Could it be that some evangelicals are swayed by love of independent action more than by earnest desire for the welfare of the people of God? And why is the evangelical movement so very tolerant of nominality in some illiterate evangelicals in Asia and Africa and so haughtily intolerant of the illiterate nominals in the Church of Rome? Could it be because nominality in my Church looks so very much less evil than nominality in your Church?

Whatever the answers to these questions may be, the time has come to recognize that all denominations (large and small, Pentecostal or Roman Catholic) do make and will make their own laws according to which they evangelize. That such evangelism and ministerial recruitment often look like raiding to other denominations is beside the point. They do happen and will continue to happen. The time has come on high theological grounds to quit fighting free persuasion, although each congregation and denomination will inevitably do all it can to hold its own members. The time has come cheerfully to admit that winning nominal members of one branch of the Church to more ardent love for Christ in another is righteous behavior. It is a duty, not a sin. It is pleasing to God. It builds the Body rather than fragments it.

In *The Faces of God*, Adrian Hastings says:

> The reestablishment of a viable visible communion of christians of the Roman Catholic, Orthodox, Anglican and Protestant traditions really is a possibility in our time—and a possibility imposing upon us an intense and continuing moral obligation . . . to seek . . . a steady growth in cooperation at all levels, but a growth which is not at this stage ordered, institutionalized or defined . . . a growth in every aspect of christian living—proclamation, . . . service, human fellowship, prayer . . . realized through the sharing of church buildings, . . . merging of pastoral structures, the sharing of retreats and theological conferences, and . . . of inter-church marriage.[3]

3. Adrian Hastings, *The Faces of God: Reflections on Church and Society* (Maryknoll, N.Y.: Orbis, 1976), p. 96.

He needs to add: And a willingness to let the other church take our members and for us to take theirs, whenever they or we offer the worshiper a more devout, biblical, or life-changing experience.

Cooperation which proceeds on the basis of permanently frozen memberships is really no cooperation. Unshakable monopoly of each denomination, no matter how cold, formal, or careless it has become in feeding its sheep and searching for the lost, guarantees death, not life. The more such monopolistic denominations cooperate, the deader they become. Loose the Churches and let them go. Encourage all Christians to the highest possible devotion to their Lord and the most instant obedience to the will of God, within whatever branch of the Church they find most life. This does not fragment the Body of Christ. This builds up the Church around Him who said, "I came that they may have life and have it more abundantly."

24

Muscle and Mission

As the Church spreads into new populations in developed and developing nations and the gospel lifts men and women into the glorious liberty of Christ, substantial resources are always involved. Discipling *ta ethnē* is not child's play, but a major operation requiring logistical support of considerable magnitude. Muscle is needed. Momentous decisions as to where to spend men and money must be made.

The Great Commission in all its many forms—Pauline, Lukan, Matthean, and Johannine—*commands* that the peoples of earth, *panta ta ethnē*, be discipled. Men and women of "every tongue and tribe and kindred and nation" ought to be evangelized. Enormous numbers are concerned. Huge populations have yet to hear and believe the Good News.

The Bible must be translated so that the three billion who have not yet heard of Christ, who have not yet read God's revelation in the canonical books, may read it. Each segment of the huge global population ought to be able to read God's Word in its own mother tongue. Even now more than two thousand small languages have yet to be blessed by having the gospel voiced by them.

Great new apartment complexes (each housing 100,000 or 250,000 souls) are yet to be churched. This will not be done by pennies.

Treasure will be required. Alluvial plains dotted thickly with villages and boasting a population of 900 unbelievers to the square mile must be brought "to obedience of faith" (Rom. 16:26). The task will not be done by dropping in for a little casual evangelism or by starry-eyed idealists resting comfortably on the thought that "the nationals will do it." Serious, well-supported, logistically sound, and long-continued labors are demanded. All this I call muscle. Getting it will require momentous, costly decisions.

The responsiveness of the peoples of earth has never been greater. In any given year thousands of small groups of non-Christians—sometimes educated, sometimes illiterate, sometimes living in cities, sometimes in forests—hear the gospel and become serious inquirers. Often they progress on through baptism to membership in a church. These groups live immersed in their cultures and kinship webs. When a group becomes Christian, it has literally thousands of kin contacts who are deeply interested that "some of our people have become Christian." Each of these good little beginnings might become a sweeping people movement, spreading the fire of faith throughout a whole *ethnos* of, let us say, half a million.

Once in a long while such a movement does develop; but typically the small group of converts increases to a few hundreds, or at most a thousand or two, and then stops. People movements that have been arrested litter the lands of earth. Many factors lead to arrest, but one is that muscle is not made available to these good little beginnings. These priceless gifts of God are not seriously developed. Making available substantial resources, trained men, and competent guidance to the most promising of these would enable many more to reach the proportions which God intended for them.

Sources of Support for Evangelism

Where will such substantial resources come from? The wealthy denominations whose members all own cars have the resources. As conscience on mission rises, they can and will give more. The key to greater giving of life and money is increased awareness that world evangelism is not merely one of many good deeds to which kindly Christians "really ought to give a little." World evangelization is commanded by God. Obeying that command, voiced in so many passages in the Bible, is required of every Christian. In the global village every Christian—every real Christian—will give substantially of his or her life and money to spread the light and multiply churches (which are lighthouses).

Then, too, mission boards could secure substantial resources by being responsible stewards. They can measure the effectiveness of every piece of mission work in terms of the great goal and withdraw resources from unproductive projects. Lessening support to those pieces of mission work which, after careful research, appear highly unlikely to spread the light will cost tears. But momentous decisions of this sort must be made if the movements that are multiplying congregations of righteous souls are to be sufficiently reinforced. This principle was illustrated by Chrysler Corporation, which, when it faced bankruptcy, closed those factories which were not productive and poured resources into those factories which made excellent cars. That was the secret of its remarkable recovery. God expects missionary societies also to use good business sense.

The Church of Jesus Christ has wealth, wisdom, and consecration, but at present is not using those resources to encourage the many small people movements God has called into being. The Church ought not to delude itself that great movements to Christ will occur without great commitments of prayer and treasure.

The indigenous-church theory is partly responsible for the casual attitude which Churches, missionary societies, schools of missions, and missionary magazines commonly exhibit. I agree with that theory and hold that the view of missions which John L. Nevius, Roland Allen, and others have taught is sound. Nevertheless, an erroneous marginal learning often accompanies the method:

> When men turn to Christ and the first few become Christians and form churches, missions must beware lest they smother the movement by too much care and too much direction. Once the movement starts, the main business of the missionary is to keep out of its way. He stands back and lets a national leadership develop. The Holy Spirit will guide the movement. If the new little beginning is a real Church, it cannot be stopped. If it fails, it was not a real Church.

Believing this error, many a Church and many a missionary society have stood by while small movements of great potential have slowed down, become gatherings of a few hundred or a few thousand, and sealed themselves off, becoming small enclaves of Christians out of contact with the bulk of their kith and kin.

This erroneous theory has proved particularly detrimental during the past thirty years, because it enabled a Church or mission to regard its small declining efforts with moral satisfaction. The indigenous-church theory became a good justification for missions which did not cost much and carried on ineffectual and soon-ended evangelization.

Careful examination of the great movements in Asia, Latin America, and Africa, through each of which several hundred thousand have come into a redemptive relationship to Jesus Christ, reveals that many of the missions assisting these movements found ways to multiply congregations led by paid trained pastors (workers, teacher-preachers, evangelists). If there was a chance to establish scores or hundreds of such congregations, that was done and the bill was paid. This is almost the diametrical opposite of the common misconception about the indigenous method—that is, "Never pay a worker in the church. Let the church expand entirely under unpaid workers. When it needs paid workers, it will (all by itself, mind you) recruit, train, ordain, and pay them." So commonly is this caricature believed that the first two sentences of this paragraph will seem wrong to many readers. Because the caricature is widely believed, many promising small movements are—with the best intentions in the world—starved or neglected. Naturally they remain small.

Once in a long while in a receptive people dissatisfaction with existing conditions is so deep rooted, a movement to Christ is so powerful, the influence of the first to become Christians so great, and their experience of the Holy Spirit so joyous, that despite neglect the movement flourishes. Congregations multiply without much attention, and the movement attains such power that it cannot be sealed off and arrested. Gradually the fathering mission starts an adequate shepherding program, and other missions come in and disciple parts of the receptive people. Once in a long while, repeated fresh starts gradually build up a sizable Church. Far from proving that muscle is *not* needed, these exceptional cases display additional ways in which resources can sometimes be created.

Ways to Create Resources

The muscle needed to start, shepherd, and extend great movements to Christ has been created in four main ways. The first and most common way has been for the mission concerned to push winning, discipling, and enrolling as fast and far as possible, and to recruit, train, pay, and direct a corps of workers who both shepherd the small growing churches and start hundreds of others. Sometimes these workers were all paid. Sometimes the corps was comprised of both paid and unpaid evangelist-teachers. When a village teacher-preacher considered a regular wage of three dollars per month (in local currency, of course) quite satisfactory, a large number of workers could be employed for a few thousand dollars a year.

The second way of creating needed resources was for the tribe becoming Christian to give the teacher-preacher tribal land on which to grow his food and small cash or kind offerings from the new little congregation. Sometimes the children taught by the teacher-preacher would pay him small fees. The function of the mission in this second case was chiefly to organize expansion. As congregations formed, the mission recruited, trained, and sent to them slightly literate pastor-teachers whose wives did the field work and grew the food. Those pastors who did not do well, the mission replaced. Those who did well, the mission promoted to supervisory responsibilities. A few of the very best the mission pushed on up the educational ladder to ordained status. In this second case, the muscle came from the multiplying congregations—organized and greatly assisted by the mission or the Church. Where tribal land is available, this is a good method.

The third way was for the government, anxious to educate the villagers, to pay teachers of new small village schools. Sometimes pay was given once a year according to the number of pupils who passed an examination conducted by the government inspector of schools. He would pay the teacher so much per pupil passed. Since few teachers could support themselves for twelve months in anticipation of getting government pay at examination time, the mission managed the system, paid each teacher a monthly wage, supervised the schools, distributed suitable books and supplies, and recouped part of the expense at examination time. In a receptive people the mission opened schools where people wanted to become Christian and where the additional expense could be justified on the basis that the teacher was also a pastor. He taught school and received three-fourths of his wage from the government. He led a small congregation, and its offerings plus mission subsidy gave him the balance of his income. Sizable resources were thus created, and great movements surged forward. I have met supervisors (sometimes missionaries and sometimes nationals) who managed two hundred small village schools!

The fourth main way has been for the movement itself to pay all its pastor-teachers. New congregations were not started, inquirers were not enrolled until they declared that they would erect a pastor's house and a church-school building and pay the pastor-teacher a living wage. When new Christian cells were started without a resident paid pastor, they were attached to a nearby church. Thus a circle pastor might have several small congregations under his care. His salary came from all of these (although the weakest contributed little), and he gave them all some shepherding. The function of the missionary in this fourth way was to train the pastors, give apostolic oversight, and encourage the movement. By "encourage" I mean visit, pray with, send the sick to hospital, pay fees for pastors' children going on to boarding school, hold annual camp meetings or other gatherings for instruction and inspiration, start Bible schools or seminaries, send a few leaders to other countries to study, and so on. All these took mission money, time, and love—in large amounts. The fourth way was seldom the beginning way. Most movements began in one of the other three ways, and as they became strong enough emerged into the fourth way.

I long believed that the great movement to Christian faith which swept through the United Presbyterian field in north India (now Pakistan) became completely self-supporting before 1900, very early in its history. But the Reverend Frederick E. Stock, co-author of *People Movements in the Punjab*, assures me that mission subsidies of various sorts constituted a substantial part of the village pastor's salary until well into the thirties. Muscle was employed.

In 1947 the Methodist Church of South India had ninety-seven thousand members. This number increased in the twenty years following to two hundred thousand. In 1967 most of the ordained ministers leading the Church were receiving a considerable part of their salary from the Methodist Church in South Asia, that is, from American mission money disbursed by the Indian Church. I am not criticizing this. On the contrary, I am commending it. Citing this fact helps prove that discipling *ta ethnē* has taken and will continue to take substantial resources. There is no cheap way to carry out the Great Commission.

To be sure, some indigenous Churches grow to power without any overseas resources at all. For example, the True Jesus Churches and the house-church movement in China have never received any money from abroad. The Iglesia Ni Cristo in the Philippines, the Congregación Cristan in Brazil, the Methodist Pentecostals in Chile, and the Kimbanguists in Zaire—to mention only a few—number from two hundred thousand to five hundred thousand members each. Some erect large, beautiful church buildings with their own funds. This does not damage my thesis in the least. Rather it supports it. These large denominations apply large amounts of muscle to the propagation of the gospel. After World War II, the Iglesia Ni Cristo (INC) sent "missionaries" (emissaries paid from the central fund, supplied with work budgets from the central fund) to multiply churches in new parts of the Philippine archipelago. When the INC erected a beautiful church seating one thousand people in Baguio, the major cost was not paid by the Christians in Baguio but by the central fund. The Congregacáon Cristan in Brazil pays no preachers. It operates entirely on the basis of an unpaid voluntary eldership. Consequently, large resources are available to construct million-dollar church buildings where the denominational leaders think they will do most to expand the Church.

The principle stands—the expansion of the Church, the spread of the gospel, does not take place of itself. It takes considerable quantities of hard cash and many dedicated Christians who pour themselves into bringing their people to faith and obedience.

The Lord of the Church, who does not desire that any should perish (although many will choose the broad way) would be pleased if His obedient servants would pour resources into good beginnings where small groups keep erupting into Christian faith. Conferences between leaders of national Churches and missionary societies would easily determine where the truest, most vigorous response lies. How to assemble substantial continuing support for truly great movements could easily be determined.

It would also please Him for any one mission or Church to measure its various opportunities and with its own money and men back the most promising. Merely doubling the resources will not accomplish this goal. Together with more adequate logistics must go more believing prayer, more adequate strategy, more godly living, more culturally suitable methods, more unselfish service—in short, more effective evangelism. "Muscle" includes all this.

The Holy Spirit's Work in World Evangelism

What is the part of the Holy Spirit in world evangelization? World evangelization is essentially a movement of the Holy Spirit. It was the Holy Spirit who sent Paul and Barnabas from Antioch to Cyprus. It is the Holy Spirit who moves all true missionaries to their work. The Holy Spirit is absolutely essential to the missionary task.

It is also true that the Holy Spirit expects those through whom He carries out His work to exercise good judgment, business acumen, and selfless sacrifice. When we speak about muscle, we are speaking about the costly decisions that the Holy Spirit calls on Christians to make. The word *muscle* indicates long-continued costly effort—spiritual, intellectual, and physical. Muscle is an ingredient of all successful discipling.

We remember the long-continued costly effort of Paul:

> Are they servants of Christ? (I speak as if insane) I more so; in far more labors, in far more imprisonments, beaten times without number, often in danger of death. Five times I received from the Jews thirty-nine lashes. Three times I was beaten with rods, once I was stoned, three times I was shipwrecked, a night and a day I have spent in the deep. I have been on frequent journeys, in dangers from rivers, dangers from robbers, dangers from my countrymen, dangers from the Gentiles, dangers in the city, dangers in the wilderness, dangers on the sea, dangers among false brethren; I have been in labor and hardship, through many sleepless nights, in hunger and thirst, often without food, in cold and exposure. Apart from such external things, there is the daily pressure upon me of concern for all the churches. [2 Cor. 11:23–28]

The Holy Spirit is the dynamic constantly moving the Church to world evangelization. As the world continues in its revolutionary changes, the Holy Spirit will thrust out new kinds of pioneers. These will blaze sacrificial trails in cooperation, flexibility, adaptability, suffering, expendability. He will prepare missionaries to be commandos. They will spend their lives recklessly in commitment to expressing love in Jesus' name.

25

Seventeen seventy-six
and the Time Lag

Fred Kline tells of finding in the periodical room of the Library of Congress a copy of the four-page *Pennsylvania Gazette* for July 4, 1776. Kline writes:

Here was the complete text of the Declaration of Independence in one of its first newspaper appearances . . . and I have never been so moved by those familiar words, "We hold these Truths to be self-evident, that all Men are created equal, that they are endowed by their Creator with certain inalienable Rights, that among these are Life, Liberty, and the Pursuit of Happiness." Reading the four-page paper, I was struck by a very great irony brought home by many of the advertisements. Here was our fundamental testament of freedom just two columns away from reward notices for runaway indentured servants and slaves, and on the back page, slaves and servants were offered for sale. . . .

The ideal had just been born. . . . yet, for almost a hundred years slavery would still be a fact of life.[1]

The time lag between espousing a new way of life and implementing it in all aspects of daily behavior is observable in every piece of the

1. Fred Kline, "Library of Congress: The Nation's Bookcase," *National Geographic* (November 1975), p. 687.

vast mosaic of mankind. The Christian, furthermore, knows that until the Lord returns, the sin and fallibility of men guarantee that all good will be achieved in imperfect measure. This is no reason to delight in evil or to justify the evil which yet remains. Christians press on doing all they believe God desires toward instituting a peaceful, righteous, and loving society. Yet the time lag (the long years between the Declaration of Independence and equal opportunity for blacks) does emphasize the need for patience. That slavery would be legal for ninety years, gross injustice would be widespread for another ninety, and grave inequities would still exist in 1976 was no reason not to publish the Declaration of Independence.

All this bears closely on the extension of the Church on new ground. As the three billion who have yet to believe hear the gospel, accept Jesus Christ as Lord and Savior, and become responsible members of His Church, clusters of congregations arise in varied segments of the population of country after country.

They form churches. Christ gave Himself up for the Church that she might be presented before him "in splendor, without spot or wrinkle or any such thing, that she might be holy and without blemish" (Eph. 5:27, RSV). That is a glorious ideal. Yet churches come in as "babes in Christ" (1 Cor. 3:1; 1 Peter 2:2) and for long years display many wrinkles, spots, and blemishes. Two columns away from the Declaration of Independence were advertisements of rewards for the return of runaway slaves!

In Zam Zam, a village far from any medical aid, a little boy lies dying. The pagan relatives and friends all know that in such circumstances one offers a black rooster to the lord of the gods, a large rock near the village; without his permission no evil spirit can remain in the village. The illiterate new Christian mother prays to God, but her little boy lies dying. She then goes with her mother-in-law to the lord of the gods and beheads the rooster. A blemish? Yes, of course. Deplorable? Yes. Displeasing to God? Certainly. But does it prove that she and her husband and the fifteen other families who became Christian ought never to have been baptized? By no means! It proves that strong, wealthy denominations and congregations ought to send far more missionaries, do far more teaching, and plan far more intelligently to cooperate with new young denominations and congregations in perfecting immature saints.

Chattel slavery in 1775 in Virginia, educational and economic slavery in the South in 1875, gross inequity in the United States in

1975, and wrinkles, imperfections, and blemishes in the Church in Zam Zam simply prove that we should press on toward implementing the ideal. Enormous numbers of first graders, who cannot add up a column of figures or read a verse of the Bible, are a most significant and heartening fact of life. Far from being reason to open no more first grades, they constitute the best reason for opening thousands more first grades. Enormous numbers of people-movement congregations full of Christians whose practice of the biblical way of life leaves much to be desired are most significant and heartening. They shout, "Press on multiplying people movement congregations like us, and rejoice that you have been counted worthy to multiply churches on new ground." Common sense teaches us the same thing.

Common sense also teaches that the first grade should be followed by the second and third, and eventually by the eleventh and twelfth. Wealthy, powerful churches have been created by God for precisely this time—that they may nurture multiplying churches; that rivers of the water of life may flow without let or hindrance; that trucks loaded with the bread of heaven may roar off across every country to feed the hungry.

Correct missionary strategy is not to whittle down the number of new churches we permit to start so that we can care for them with our present small resources. Correct policy is not to pontificate against people movements and postulate that Christians brought in by them are not "real" Christians. Right strategy rather rejoices that, as in no other era of history, new congregations can be born and, indeed, are being born. The mighty resources of Christ's Church should be engaged in multiplying congregations by every means possible, and then in weaning the babes and feeding them solid food. Literature, radio, television, air travel, modern medicine, printing, mimeographing, enormous quantities of social, economic, and political information, the Bible in hundreds of languages, Bible translators by the thousands, 100,000 congregations in India and 320,000 in the United States which can be geared for church multiplication—all testify to the power God has placed in the hands of His Church. To whom much has been given, from him much is expected.

Let us lay to rest the tired excuse that beginning imperfections are reasons for inaction. Of course, most congregations forming on new ground manifest a time lag between what they should be and what they are. The congregation at Corinth was typical in that aspect. This did not, however, deter Paul from furiously multiplying new congregations around Ephesus and planning to multiply congregations in Spain. Imperfect new congregations, like first grades, are a cause for exultation, renewed dedication, and a mighty gearing of the churches for mission.

A wonderful example of what can be and must be done comes from China in the 1970s. There the Three-Self Churches, which had been planted by missionaries during the nineteenth and early twentieth centuries, were being heavily repressed, confined, and persecuted by the communist government. They were not multiplying new churches. However, radio broadcasts from outside China were reaching enormous numbers of Chinese, particularly in rural sections. Many Chinese, observing that communism had not really improved their lot very much, listened to the gospel with joy. They formed groups which listened to the radio broadcasts in secret. They searched for and found Bibles, New Testaments, and Gospels which had been secreted by existing Christians. They copied sections of these by hand. House fellowships of those who believed in Christ and studied His Word began to multiply. House churches, meeting in secret, began to appear all over China. Some consisted of five families, some of fifty. Some met in fields and some in the dead of night in homes.

Today reliable reports from visitors to China put the number of house-church Christians at twenty million, fifty million, seventy-five million, or one hundred million. Under communist government no certain count is possible, but we may be sure that there has been an explosive growth in the number of practicing Christians.

Christian radio, literature, and motion pictures (mass-media ministries) in all unreached populations have considered their task that of proclaiming Christ—no more. Today, under the impact of the Chinese example, they are beginning to say, "In addition to proclaiming Christ, let us invite listeners to form groups of believers. These may be called Christ groups, home fellowships, Bible-study groups, or house churches. They will arise beyond the reach of existing churches."

True, these new fellowships of believers will not follow the tactics of any existing denomination. They will read the Bible or even one Gospel and worship the Lord Jesus Christ. Their understanding will probably be somewhat faulty. But if the invitation stresses that all other gods and all other religious books must be put aside, they will have started on the Christian path. They can be encouraged to proceed. They have enrolled in grade 1, or, as the English say, in standard 1. They have signed a declaration of independence. They believe that all men are created equal. There will be a time lag before this basic principle is fully carried out in their lives and incorporated in their social structures. That this time lag exists is no reason to oppose or bewall the signing of their declaration of independence. That such house fellowships, groups that listen to broadcasts, Christ groups, or house churches are imperfect may be taken for granted. But that is no reason to oppose their formation.

Readers will at once think of many other examples which fit urban populations, rural populations, illiterate populations, highly literate populations, and the like. These differ in every country. Beginning churches will suffer under many handicaps. The handicaps must not be allowed to stop church planting, although, of course, every effort must be made—and will be made—to mature beginning churches as rapidly as possible. Grade 1 will be followed by grades 2, 3, and 4.

As missionary societies, missionaries, denominations, and mass-media ministries resolve to multiply their efforts at world evangelization, this time lag calls for many momentous decisions. For example, the missionary society, while working hard at perfecting the churches it has planted, must commit even greater resources to multiplying new churches. Unless missionary societies bring many new babes to birth, they will get very few mature vigorous churches.

Since nearly all the resources of most missionary societies now go to helping the denominations they have founded, momentous and costly decisions will be required to channel existing resources to unreached populations and to raise new resources for such populations. A missionary society which is spending one hundred thousand dollars to help a younger Church it fathered must now say to it, "From now on you will receive forty-five thousand dollars, and we shall send fifty-five thousand dollars to carry out frontier evangelism in populations you cannot reach. We believe that you will use a good share of this money in encouraging and supporting your own frontier evangelism. The Great Commission bears as heavily on you as it does on us. So, brethren, let us go forward together making the gospel known to all segments of society."

Any such decision will be costly, painful, and tremendously rewarding.

26

New Strategies in Missions Today

A bewildering series of new emphases has marked mission during the past thirty years. The latest is an emphasis on mankind's thirst for a true word about God. This basic need has been overlooked in much recent missiological writing. The most weakening and demeaning of all hungers is that which rages in the souls of men who do not know God. When men and women believe themselves to be merely higher animals, they fall prey to all kinds of assaults on human dignity.

But when men have a clear authoritative word from the everlasting God, the Creator of the universe, the God of Abraham, Isaac, and Jacob, the God and Father of Our Lord Jesus Christ, Judge of the nations, *then*, whatever the external circumstances, they live like men and, when the time comes, they die like men. *Then* women, knowing themselves to be daughters of the King, live fully human lives. Degrading value systems, cultural components, and standards of achievement are recognized and lose their power. Strengthened by the powerful proteins of divine purpose, individual believers resolutely work to institute social improvements.

Those who feed on the Word of God form criteria of judgment based on the models of life which God has approved. To use Paul's metaphor, they seek the things that are above. They recognize things below as transient. Not as unreal, mind you. God's Word does not teach that the world round about us is illusory. It is real, but transient.

Christians should feed the physically hungry and clothe the physically naked and should look after their own families' earthly welfare, too. But they do this as pilgrims. They do this as servants of the King. The same King who commands them to feed the physically hungry commands them to distribute the Bread of Heaven and to disciple *panta ta ethnē*. There is no surer way permanently to alleviate poverty, injustice, and oppression than to lead non-Christians to Christ and to help them become practicing Christians. Then these populations will have the power to act in just, peaceful, and brotherly ways.

These abilities are born out of the experience of redemption. They are empowered by the divine Guest who now lives in the house. They cannot rise out of animality or earthy humanity. They are part of the new creation. They make true human dignity possible. In darkness they make us want to seek the light. In want, they draw us to strengthening food. In dryness, they lead us to the living water. In filth, they make us crave cleanliness. In mortality, they are intimations of eternal life.

The world in which we live is a welter of conflicting standards. Some shout that there is no standard. Whatever anyone wants to do is right. Whatever the culture demands must be done. Do what feels good to you, they urge.

Some, seeing the bankruptcy of this moral and religious relativism, urge sociological consensus as the basis for morality. Sociological consensus in those few societies where multitudes accept God's Word as ultimate authority has a semblance of value; but in most societies sociological consensus simply gives an appearance of solidity to the quicksand—like a dry crust over a dangerous bog. Some make idols of this god and that, of the human spirit, or of men's ability to solve problems. They proclaim each value system and each religion or ideology as if it were ultimate truth. That what each says concerning ultimate reality cancels what others are saying appears not to trouble superficial thinkers.

Serious minds, however, finding no truth anywhere, come to the gloomy conclusion that there is no truth. All that exists is the play of circumstances, a world of chance, with the human race merely the present outcome of a very remarkable sequence of atomic accidents.

There is no ultimate right. There is no ultimate wrong. All there is, is what, given this set of circumstances and this arrangement of power, is expedient. If you have the power, whatever you do is right. Moral anarchy is the intellectual ground for much of contemporary life. That it does not appear as anarchy is due chiefly to the fact that the Christian framework still shines through the multitudinous contradictions. Even when men deny the special revelation and refuse to see the general revelation, they are influenced by both. Hitler, Mussolini, Mao, and Attila the Hun are routinely denounced by the very people who, were it not for the Christian revelation, would speedily emulate them.

What new strategies in mission does all this require? We must develop a growing sense that above everything else, peoples of Europe, America, and the third world need to accept a sure word about God. People by people they ought consciously to yield to Christ, intelligently accept the Bible as God's self-disclosure, the only rule of faith and practice, and actively participate in Christ's Body the Church. We must devise strategies which fit contemporary situations and intend to increase these convictions.

This new emphasis means that the world mission of the Church must be seen as calling men and women from the darkness of agnosticism, Secularism, and false gods to the light of the world. It means ministering to the needs of men, not as wolves sharing the bloody meat they have just dragged down, but as members of God's household helping other members. When the King's daughters help a starving princess, they are conscious that if a princess thinks she is an animal or merely a human being, no amount of soup is going to do her any lasting good. She needs to realize she also is a daughter of the King. This new emphasis means that leading men and women and whole *ethnē* to follow Christ constitutes the heart of Christian mission. Much else will be done. Transient needs must be met. Pilgrims must eat. Life is complex. But if everything else is done and this is not, Christian mission has not been carried out.

This new emphasis means that congregations, denominations, brotherhoods, unions, and synods ought to recognize that communicating the truth about the transcendent God and His revealed will is the heart of Christian mission. They ought to make costly decisions to allocate their resources to this end. Billions of men and women have yet to believe on Christ, know Him, love Him, and follow Him in the fellowship of His Church. Churches ought to spend their money so the tremendous hunger of humankind for a sure word about God is met.

As far as the missionary movement, the evangelization of the world, is concerned, this newest emphasis in missions is also the oldest. It animated the Jerusalem Church, the Antioch Church, and the patristic Church. It has underghded and inspired every great expansion of Christianity from that day to this. Consequently, the congregations and denominations now existing and all new units of the Church as they are born should share in this basic biblical conviction to make Christ known, loved, and obeyed. Mission should encourage men and women as individuals and as social units to become His reliable and trustworthy followers. This is the heart of Christian mission and an essential part of the divine life which flows in every true Church.

Evangelical missions have been emphasizing this for years. It is not for them a new thing. Many Christian organizations have been marching to the beat of this drum. But other great currents of mission thought in the six continents in the past two decades have been flowing in other directions. What is new is that now some of them, too, are recognizing the continuing heart of Christian mission and are devising strategies to multiply this mind among all Christians.

Truly a new wind is blowing. New strategies in mission must be devised to bring winning the world for Christ back to the center of all mission action. New strategies in mission must not be limited to using certain new technologies such as radio, moving pictures, theological education by extension, and the like; nor to new insights derived from the sciences of communication, anthropology, and sociology. Much more important than any of these is the new recognition that the discipling of *panta ta ethnē* is both the command of God and the best thing that can be done for mankind.

Index